THE DRIFTER

Salem was a rich town in a rich territory and it all belonged to Neal Shute. He had won Salem with his fists and guns, and he ruled it the same way.

Until the Drifter, Pete Dannifer, came to town. First he disappeared with the girl, Tammy, for days. Then he tried to take over Shute's empire.

Only one thing would satisfy Shute now—to kill Dannifer with his bare hands.

A RUTHLESS ACTION WESTERN NOVEL
BY WILL COOK

Bantam Books by Will Cook

THE DRIFTER
by Will Cook

THE DRIFTER
A Bantam Book | January 1969
2nd printing .... February 1979

ISBN 0-553-12404-8

Published simultaneously in the United States and Canada

Bantam Books are published by Bantam Books, Inc. Its trademark, consisting of the words "Bantam Books" and the por-
trayal of a bantam, is Registered in U.S. Patent and Trademark
Office and in other countries. Marca Registrada. Bantam
Books, Inc., 666 Fifth Avenue, New York, New York 10019.

PRINTED IN THE UNITED STATES OF AMERICA

THE DRIFTER

Chapter 1

As soon as she woke, Tammy McCain realized that the rain
had stopped, and she got out of bed and went to the window
and looked at the gray dawn. She could see only a few
clouds, and to the east the sun was a pink haze behind the
Cascade Range; it would be a good day, a day for doing all
those outside things that had had to be put off.

She dressed and brushed her hair and could hear her
mother stirring in the cabin's big room. Then her younger
brother slammed out to fetch the morning water, and her father said something to him, as he always did when he de-
tected some lack of consideration for others.

The mirror to her dresser had been broken on the way
west, so she stood by the window, catching a faint reflection
of herself in the glass as she tied a ribbon in her hair. There
were times when she felt that her life was hard, for the summers were hot and the insects were bad and the work never
ended; but then she saw the other families in the valley and
she thought that perhaps her life was better than theirs. The
indecision gnawed at her, for at eighteen she hadn't quite
learned to make up her mind about anything and stick to it.

She left her small room and went into the kitchen; her
mother was at the stove frying meat and potatoes. Tammy
stepped to the door. The grass, in the first bland light of the
sun, was wet and clean, and there was snow on some of the
higher peaks of the Cascades. It was early for snow, but she
was glad to see it, for it would drive the game down and keep
the Indians busy, and a body wouldn't need to worry about
them stealing a cow or making trouble.

Her brother Quincy came across the yard with the water
buckets, and he playfully swung one at her. She stepped back
quickly.

"Don't you get me wet," she said.

"You won't melt," he said laughing, and went on into the
kitchen.

1

Angus McCain's firm voice said, "Don't pester your sister, boy."

"Heck," Quincy said, "everything I do is a pester." He was big for his fourteen years, with a thick mane of hair and the devil in his eyes. He resembled his father strongly.

"I can use help," Mrs. McCain said, meaning it for Tammy.

"You always can," Tammy said, and turned from the door.

"And I always get your sass too, don't I?"

The anger surprised Tammy, for she hadn't meant anything at all. She started to say something back, because it was hard not to, only this time she held it and went to the stove and tended the frying meat. She shot a sidelong glance at her mother and saw the anger still there on her face. She didn't understand any of it and really didn't care to; it was easier to let a thing go in one ear and out the other.

By turning slightly, she could see her father at the table. He was a big man who just could not be hurried, yet he always seemed to finish well ahead of faster men. Four years now in the valley, and already his place was better than any of the others. They had glass in the windows; he'd bought it in Salem, exactly as many panes as he needed, and won a ten-dollar gold piece from Neal Shute, who had bet him he couldn't get them thirty miles down the valley without breaking any. It was, Tammy supposed, all part of her father's calculation—to make the bet and win it, and that way get the glass for nothing. He was by nature a shrewd man to dicker with.

Tammy set the table, and when the meat was cooked she took her place by her brother and Angus McCain said Grace: "Dear Lord, bless this food and this house. Keep us free of sin. And keep the pesky Injuns out of the valley this winter. Amen."

He was not a man who talked at the table; food was fuel to him, and eating a chore to be finished as quickly as possible. Only when he started to drink his coffee did he say anything now: "How does this morning find you, Essie?"

"Poorly," Mrs. McCain said, "but it could be the weather. I get flashes now and then."

"What ails you, ma?" Quincy said.

She became angry again, her face set. "Never you mind. It's no concern of yours, anyway."

"There's no need to get mad at him," Tammy said.

Her mother turned her head quickly and snapped, "I'll get

mad when I please!" Then she pressed her knuckles to her lips and sat there, her eyes growing red.

"Tammy, clear the table," Angus McCain said. "Quincy, milk the no-horn cow." He waited until they got up, then touched his wife on the arm. "Why don't you gather the eggs, Essie? You don't fluster the hens."

"I seem to fluster everyone else," she said, and got up.

She got her shawl and basket and went out, and a moment later Angus McCain followed. Tammy could see him crossing the yard to the barn to begin his work. She washed the dishes and dried them and put them away, and then she made the beds.

She was back in the kitchen when her mother came in with the eggs. "They're laying poorly," she said. "Must be the weather. Does it have to rain all the time? I never seen such rain. In Ohio it wasn't like this. It'd rain and quit, but here it rains as if it'll never quit." She looked at Tammy. "You listenin' to me?"

"I guess I wasn't," Tammy said.

That brought the stiffness back to her mother's face, and Tammy was sorry; sorry that she'd started it all again. "I'll make the beds," Mrs. McCain said.

"They're made, ma."

"What's the matter—didn't you think I could do it?"

"I didn't think that at all," Tammy said. She went over and took her mother by the arm. "Nothing I do makes you happy, ma. I don't want it that way." When her mother just stood there without speaking, Tammy dropped her hand. "All right, ma."

"It ain't all right. Nothin's right any more." Her mother's hands came together and she twisted her fingers. "It's getting so a body can't look out the window without seein' some fella comin' here for a drink at the spring and a look at you."

Tammy stared, and it seemed to anger her mother, this denial, even though it was silent. "Don't say it ain't so. And don't tell me you don't smile and invite 'em back with your eyes."

"All right! You want me to be a grouch like you?"

"You'll turn into no haystack tramp around here!"

They stood there, staring at each other in silence, realizing what they were saying. Then Tammy said, "I'm goin' over to the Wilkerson place today. She's coming to her time."

"Tammy, why do we always say things like we do?"

"I don't know, ma. I guess you don't either," Tammy said, and went into the bedroom for her things. She rolled up two blankets and an extra dress, and when she came out her mother was standing there. "Neal Shute might drop by tomorrow," Tammy said. "Tell him where I am."

"It would seem," Mrs. McCain said, "that a man's business would keep him more to home. Salem's a far piece for a man to ride when there's the promise of nothin' on the other end. Or has there been?"

"Think what you want," Tammy said, and turned away.

"You hold foot and answer me!"

"What's there to answer, ma?" Tammy said. "You've made up your mind and there's no changin' it."

"I don't want to think those things," her mother said. "But you don't talk to me no more, Tammy."

Tammy looked at her, a bulky, gray-haired woman made old by never-ending work, and she felt sorry for her. "Ma, I'll stay at the Wilkerson place a few days. You won't miss me."

"I will, Tammy. I will."

"We're just not gettin' along, ma. Wouldn't it be better if we both come out and admitted it?" She lifted her shoulders in a slight shrug. "We just don't get anywhere with this. Every day's the same."

Mrs. McCain brushed hair away from her forehead. "I want you to stop thinkin' the things you're thinkin' all the time," she said. "I want you to stop moonin', and find a nice man and marry and raise a family. You've got to settle your mind, Tammy. You're a grown woman."

"Do you really think so? Good-bye, ma."

"Good-bye?" Her mother looked as though she were on the edge of panic. "Don't say it like that, Tammy!"

"I just said it plain like. Ma, I'm only goin' seven miles down the road."

She picked up her bundle and left the cabin and walked toward the barn. Her father stopped his work when she came up. He was a bearded man who smiled with his eyes. She was his favorite, and he found it hard to see her faults, or even admit that she had any at all.

"Goin' today?" he asked.

She nodded. "I got to go, pa. Sometimes I think I've got to go and keep on goin'."

"It's a disease of the young," he said. "I ran away from home eight times before I was fifteen. The ninth time I kept on goin'." He paused. "Your mother's to that age when things bother her easy. You've got to understand and overlook a lot."

"It ain't easy," Tammy said.

"Tolerance is hard any time," Angus McCain said. "What'll I tell Neal Shute when he comes around?"

"Tell him to ride over if he's a mind. If he's ridden this far, a little more won't hurt him."

McCain frowned, but he spoke pleasantly. "You're takin' advantage of bein' a woman, Tammy. Neal's a proud man. A bit jealous too, and quick of temper. It's no good to rile a man needlessly." He put his arm around her. "This spring you prodded the Kuntz boy into trouble."

"He picked his fight," Tammy said.

McCain shook his head. "But it was your smile that told him to pick it. Neal hurt that boy. He ain't quite right in the head now, and it's gotten some folks to talkin'."

"What hurt can talk do?"

"It can take the livin' out of life," McCain said. He looked at her bundle. "You've got your own blankets? Good. The Wilkersons are hard put as it is, and it wouldn't be right to impose. Stay on the road and away from the river; God knows who'll you'll meet travelin' it. Don't wander and take a short cut. The Injuns have been quiet, but Lord knows it takes little to set 'em off." She nodded and he looked at her, not at all sure that she would obey him. "You'll be careful?"

"Yes," she said, and turned toward the pasture; she'd climb the fence to the road rather than use the gate. McCain called after her: "Have Wilkerson send up smoke when you get there. I'll send Quincy to the hilltop this afternoon to watch."

She waved her hand; it was her answer, and he picked up his manure fork, meaning to begin his work again. Then he saw his wife standing in the cabin door, and her attitude, the way she stood, made him put the fork down and go to her. As he reached the cabin door he said, "Is there any coffee left, Essie?"

She nodded and went in with him and got a cup and saucer.

"I wouldn't spend too much time worrying about her, was I you, Essie," he said. He waited until she had poured the coffee and sat down across from him. "She's got her own mind and means to use it. It's the things we taught her that count now. What we say won't do much good."

"I don't understand her none at all," she said. "It's as if I'd raised a stranger. Or maybe I've become a stranger to myself, Angus." She shook her head. "Sometimes I think it would be better if we'd settled in town."

"I'm not a town man," he said. "Never was, never will be. We've got a good life, Essie." He reached out and took her hand. "We've made it good. Tammy will be all right. It'll do her good to get away for a few days—a different place, and someone else's troubles beside her own." He got up and patted his wife on the cheek. "You're goin' to let worry make an old woman of you. You don't want that."

"If I only felt better—"

"When I go to Salem the next time, I'll ask Doc Mandeley if there's a tonic you can take," McCain said. He bent and kissed her quickly, and then went out to his work, a frown gathering on his face as he left the cabin.

He searched the field with his eyes, but Tammy was gone, and he picked up his manure fork to work. Nothing, it seemed, was quite right any more; and he couldn't do anything about it; it was the first time in his life that he'd really felt this way, and it bothered him.

McCain didn't like to think of his wife changing, or of anything changing, but the past few years had brought increasingly difficult days—days when she snapped at him, or cried over something he had done, or grew sullen and silent. It wasn't a good thing, McCain thought, to be like that, and he made up his mind to fetch the doctor the next time he went to Salem. He hated to call the man so far, but it was a thing he couldn't put off now.

He wished he'd talked more with Tammy before she'd left; the girl needed an understanding word. But the trouble was that he didn't understand any more than she did. None of this bothered Quincy; he'd take his gun and go into the woods for the day, and when he came back the storm would have blown over. But Tammy couldn't do that—she was in the house all the time.

It's hell to be young, McCain thought. Hell to be old, too.

Chapter 2

In Oregon in 1858, the woods always began where the farm ended, for a farm was land cleared from the woods. Tammy climbed the fence, stopped for a moment, then cut through the timber toward the road. Her mother did not like this timber country, and Tammy could not understand why; she liked the deep shadows beneath the trees and the sharp tang of the forest, and the flowers and ferns and patches of soft grass. She liked the silence, the absence of man-made noises; yet the woods were full of sound—the sound of insects and small animals moving about, and occasionally of a bear in a tree trying to get at wild honey, or a buck leaving his bed at some disturbance.

When she reached the road she walked along it for two miles, then sat down in the grass at the base of a tall pine. Birds called and wheeled through the high trees; there was shade everywhere, and a humid, fragrant odor. She found it good to be going somewhere, even if it was only to the Wilkerson place; it was the change she wanted, a chance to get away from home.

That was an odd thing, because she could remember how it was in Iowa where she had visited relatives and longed to be back home; now the feeling was reversed and her home was something she wanted to get away from. Had she been a boy it would have been different; she would have left a year ago, but a girl couldn't do that. Only marriage would properly remove her from her home, and that was a step she wasn't sure she wanted to take.

She closed her eyes and slept a while. When she woke and went on down the road the feeling of restlessness was still with her. It bothered her, to have her mother worrying all the time, fretting all the time, and it bothered her more to know that she was the cause of it, especially when she didn't want to be the cause of anything. She tried to understand her mother, but her youth and impatience and restlessness were all against that; she could only feel a growing frustration, and an awful desire to say everything she wanted to say, and then leave.

Her mother kept telling her that she ought to get a proper man, and yet when men came around she acted stiff and suspicious, and kept watching Tammy as though she didn't trust her at all. Smiling at a man was too bold. Speaking first was too forward. Allowing a man to hold her close while dancing was improper. And if she didn't smile, she was acting petulant. If she didn't speak, she was shy. If she sat out the dance, she was too retiring.

It seemed to Tammy that there was just no pleasing her at all, and she had half a mind to stop trying.

Another mile or so down the road she came to a rise, and stopped. Ahead of her, sitting under a tree, was a man. His horse was tied nearby, and a pack horse grazed near a berry thicket. He had a small fire going, and he looked up as she came toward him.

If he was surprised to see her, he let no sign of it show.

She could see what he was doing, and she stopped to watch him. He had three kittens reeking with skunk smell. Two were tied up with strands taken from his rope; the other was gently held between his knees and he fed it broth from his tin cook-pot, using a hollow reed for a straw.

He said, "You could lend a hand."

"They stink," Tammy said.

"Yep," the man said. He was young—in his twenties; she could see that he was tall, with straight dark hair. His clothes were mostly leather; his pants were horsehide, as was his jacket. He carried a holstered revolver, not a common thing in Oregon.

"Why are you feeding the cats?" Tammy asked.

"They're blind 'cause a skunk peed on 'em."

"I don't recall seein' you around here," Tammy said.

"Just passin' through on my way to Salem," the man said. "I heard these kittens howlin' in the brush. They must have run smack dab into a skunk. It sure knocked out their smellers so's they can't find their ma."

"Won't they ever be able to see again?" Tammy asked, saddened by the thought of them going blind.

"Oh, in a day or two they'll be all right," he said. "You got a name? I'm Pete Dannifer."

"Tammy McCain. My father's farm's down the road a piece. I'm going to the Wilkersons. You must have passed it."

He frowned. "That shack about three miles back?"

"That's the Shotten place," Tammy said. "The Wilkerson cabin is farther on."

"I recall it," Dannifer said. "Didn't stop though, cause' I was in a hurry."

"You don't seem to be in much hurry now," said Tammy.

He shrugged. "I couldn't let 'em die, could I?" He took the kitten he held between his knees and tied it up, then started to feed another one. "Everything's got a right to grow to full size. Whatever happens then is going to happen anyway." He looked at her. "We all got to have our chance, don't we?"

"I guess so," Tammy said.

He laughed softly. "How come you're alone? Where's your man?"

"I don't have any. Besides, what's to hurt me? The Injuns ain't been in the valley all summer. And I know everyone around here."

"You don't know me," Dannifer said. "However, you don't have to be scared."

"I ain't," Tammy said.

He studied her a moment. "No, I guess you ain't." Then he went on, "I rode up from Texas to have a look around."

"How long did that take?"

"A year," he said, as though it didn't matter much. "It's good country. I like it." He looked at her frankly and said, "Well, you won't be long without a man. You're pretty."

"I got callers," Tammy said. "Two or three, in fact." She squatted by the side of the road. "I guess I'd let you call on me too."

He shook his head. "Pete Dannifer never stops long enough to call."

"You stopped for them scrawny cats." His offhand rejection irritated her. "What do you carry that pistol for? Do you rob stages?"

Dannifer laughed. "A couple of times when I didn't have any money I've thought of it. I just come from a country where a pistol is part of bein' dressed. Got another in my saddlebag, if you want to know. Any more questions?"

"Have you ever seen the ocean?"

"Yep. Both of 'em."

"What's it like?"

It wasn't a casual question; he sensed that, so he thought a moment before he answered. "For a while you just stand there and look at it; it's so blamed big you just can't believe there's anything at all beyond it. A man can see rivers like the Ol' Miss and be pretty impressed, but when he sees the ocean he just stands there with his jaw dropped. The air's cold and there's a smell to the sea that you'll never find on land. And the sea's got moods like a woman—sometimes it's calm and light, and other times dark and raging, but it's never the same. At first you think it is, but it ain't; there's always a difference there, and pretty soon you can tell it."

She sat down on the patch of grass beside the road. "Tell me about the things you've seen and the places you've been."

"Been to New York City," Dannifer said. "They've got paved streets and cement sidewalks. When it rains, you can walk around and not get your boots muddy. San Francisco is plumb wild. I stayed there two weeks and got out. When it gets dark a man needs eyes in the back of his head, or he'll wind up on some ship bound for around the world."

He changed cats. "Don't know how this broth is goin' to set on their stomachs. All I had was some jerked meat and flour."

Tammy raised her knees and wrapped her arms around them. "What are you goin' to do with the cats? Turn 'em loose?"

Pete Dannifer shook his head. "Some varmint would get 'em before the day was out. I guess I'll have to take 'em along. Somebody'll give 'em a home. There's a place for everybody, you know."

"Do you really think so?"

"Sure I do," Dannifer said. He cocked his head a minute, listening, then the rumble of a wagon approaching grew more distinct; in a few minutes it appeared around a jog in the road. The driver was a young man in his late teens; when he saw them he hauled up.

"Whatcha doin' here, Miss Tammy?"

"Sittin'," she said.

He looked at her and swallowed, and pushed his hat to the back of his head. "I kin see that," he said. He looked at Pete Dannifer. "What you doin', mister?"

"Feedin' cats."

He swallowed again. "I kin see that too."

"Then we can't tell you nothin' you don't know," Dannifer said.

"What you hauling, Muley?" Tammy asked.

"Some beans. Some potatoes too." He grinned. "Pa's lettin' me go all the way to Salem."

"That's something," Tammy said. "I never knew you were

allowed to go so far." She looked at Dannifer as though measuring his reaction to all this.

"Pa's got some travelers on his land," Muley said. "Down by the river. He was too busy to go."

Dannifer frowned. "Travelers? You mean them gypsies? Friend, they'll steal you blind and cut your throat afterward. You'd better tell folks along the way and in town, so they can get set to run 'em out."

Muley thought about this, then said, "I don't know. Pa said to keep my mouth shut and mind my own business." He shook his head. "I'd better mind pa, 'cause he gets plenty riled at me as it is."

Tammy glanced at Dannifer and tapped her finger against her temple.

Muley looked hurt. "Now, you didn't have to do that, Tammy. Dang it anyhow, if people'd just stop doin' that, strangers wouldn't notice at all. My pa, first thing when anyone drops in, he tells 'em I ain't all there. Dang, but that do make me mad. Sometimes I get the yearnin' to hit him."

He frowned and looked at his big, awkward hands; he had just expressed a thought that he had been forbidden even to think, and it bothered him, made him unsure of himself. "I guess it does take me longer than most to figure a thing out, but dang it, there ain't no better farmer in the valley than me. Ain't that right, Tammy?"

"That's right, Muley." She glanced at Pete Dannifer. "He farms for his pa. His pa loafs."

Dannifer nodded. "There's nothing a lazy man likes better than a big son. How come they call you Muley? That your real name?"

"Name's Marvin, but nobody calls me that. Ma used to, but she's dead."

"I hear he got that name when he was eight," Tammy said. "His pa worked him like a mule."

"That's right," Muley said. "I was too dumb to go to school."

He kept looking at the kittens. "How come you're feedin' 'em, mister?"

"A skunk peed on 'em," Tammy said.

Muley's heavy lips formed a silent O, then he said, "I don't think you ought to talk that way, Tammy. I ain't allowed to use dirty words. I know 'em all right, but I ain't allowed to say 'em." He grinned widely. "Sometimes, when I'm by myself, I cuss a little, just to get the hang of it."

He looked at the kittens again. "Whatcha gonna do with the cats, mister?"

"Find a home for 'em," Dannifer said.

Muley Shotten thought about this, then he said, "Be two days before I reach Salem. Could I have 'em? I'd take good care of 'em."

"They'd have to be hand-fed," Dannifer said.

"I'd do that," Muley promised. "A man needs somethin' of his very own. I've got nothin'." He smiled. "I'd take good care of the cats, mister."

"He would," Tammy said. "He's good with animals. Real good."

"I'd say he was good with a lot of things," Dannifer said, and handed the kittens to Muley Shotten. Muley made a bed for them between his feet, using a burlap sack.

He grinned again. "I sure do thank you, mister." He looked at Tammy. "I thank you too, Tammy."

"What for?"

He thought a minute. "Fer sayin' good about me, I guess." He clucked to the team and drove on.

Pete Dannifer watched until the wagon topped the rise and pulled out of sight. Then he kicked out his fire, put away his pot, and got ready to mount up. Tammy McCain watched him, and Dannifer said, "I'll ride you a piece down the road."

"You ain't going in the right direction," she said.

"One's as good as the other," he said. "Save you a spell of walking, if you ain't afraid to straddle a horse."

"I guess I ain't," she said, and let him boost her onto the horse. She hiked her dress immodestly and he tried not to look at her bare knees. Then she put a hand on his shoulder. "If you're in such an all-fired hurry, why are you doin' this?"

"Maybe I want another look at those gypsies camped on the Shotten place."

He mounted, and she put her arms around his waist and he gigged the horse with his heels. He could tell by the way she sat the horse that she hadn't ridden much, but he said nothing about it.

When they reached the Shotten place there was no one in sight, and Dannifer rode on for almost a mile. Then he pulled up sharply when the road made a quick bend. Two men and a woman stood in the road, and one of the men reached out and took hold of the bit and held Dannifer's horse. Both men, dark and incredibly dirty, were dressed in bright clothes. Dannifer saw no firearms, but each man wore a long knife.

"You are in a hurry?" the man said. "Stop and let the wife of Romaine tell your future."

"I can tell your future right now," Dannifer said, "if you don't let go."

Romaine smiled, and Dannifer's hand went to the butt of his pistol and he cocked it, the dry, impersonal clicks of the hammer loud in the forest quiet. The smile on the gypsy's face faded and a smoulder of anger grew in his eyes; slowly he released the hold he had on Dannifer's horse and stepped back.

"You are unfriendly."

"Ain't I though," Dannifer said, and touched his horse with his spurs. Twenty yards down the road he looked back, then took his hand away from his pistol.

"What did they want?" Tammy asked.

"Anything they thought they could get away with," Dannifer said. "From cheating you out of a dollar, to kidnaping. I'll drop you where you're goin', then ride on back. You think Muley will spread the word?"

"No," she said. "He's too used to mindin' his pa."

"Too bad. Someone ought to have a word with Shotten for lettin' them camp on his land."

"He's a hard man to talk to," Tammy said.

When they drew near the Wilkerson place, the man came out to meet them and he carried his rifle; he seemed relieved to see Pete Dannifer.

"Don't know who you are, mister, but I'm glad you're here."

Dannifer got down and lifted Tammy to the ground. "What's the matter?"

"I had prowlers last night. Stole three chickens and a hog." He shifted his rifle to the crook of his arm. "I was hopin' the pesky Injuns would stay out of the valley, but—"

"It wasn't Indians," Dannifer said. "Gypsies."

Wilkerson frowned. He was a man near thirty, a lean, hard man trying to make a go of seventy cleared acres. "What are they?"

"Some kind of foreigner," Dannifer said. "They got no homes, just roam around, stealin' and pickin' up what they can. There's a camp of 'em on Shotten's place. They must have been on the river and come ashore there."

"You seem to know your way about. But I ain't seen you

before," Wilkerson said, and introduced himself. They shook hands.

"Tammy pointed out the places to me," Dannifer said. "We gonna stand out here all day?"

Wilkerson's face turned red. "I got better manners, mister, but it's just that I'm a bit nervous and a little mad. I couldn't afford to lose that sow or the chickens, and I can't leave the place with my wife near her time." He took Dannifer by the arm. "Come in, there's coffee on. I'll put your horse in the lean-to." He took the reins of the saddle horse and the lead rope to the pack horse, which stood ten feet behind. "You want your saddlebags and bedding?"

"I'll sleep in the lean-to," Dannifer said. "Someone ought to be outside tonight, and as long as they're in the country."

"Sure am glad to see a man," Wilkerson said.

Tammy went into the house and Dannifer walked to the lean-to with Ora Wilkerson. "Been here four years," Wilkerson was saying. "Can't tell if I've made any progress or not. How does a man tell?"

"You've built well," Dannifer said, putting the horses in the lean-to. He saw no other animals there, and he remarked about it.

"My cow pulled her pin day before yesterday and went over to the Shotten place." He shook his head. "I ain't had time to go fetch her, to tell the truth. And I kind of thought the old man would send Muley over with her." He grinned a little. "A mistake, to be sure. It ain't like the old man to go out of his way for anyone."

"I'll fetch your cow," Dannifer said, and he took his horse out again, mounted up. "Want to talk to Shotten anyway." He left before Wilkerson could stop him, and loped back along the trail the way he had come.

Chapter 3

When he reached the place where Romaine had stopped him, he put his hand on the butt of his pistol, expecting trouble, but the gypsy was gone and Dannifer went on.

He turned in at the Shotten place. The old man came out of

the cabin to meet him, but he stood by the door as if there were a rifle there that he could reach in a hurry.

"What do you want?" Shotten asked. He was a bluff, whiskered man, tall and heavy and dark-skinned.

"Wilkerson's cow," Dannifer said.

Shotten's eyes widened a bit, then he laughed. "Can't the man come after his own animal?"

"His wife's come to her time," Dannifer said. "I'm just doin' the man a favor."

"Do yourself a favor and get out," Shotten said. "I don't like people on my place."

Dannifer was facing the doorway and Shotten was commanding his attention, but he caught the slight movement out of the corner of his eye, caught the bit of color of a man's arm drawn back, and he let his instincts take over—the instincts bred into him from Indian fighting and a generation of Texas violence. He dropped to the left side of the saddle and Romaine's knife missed him by a scant distance, then Dannifer fired his pistol through the open bottom of the holster, the .44 bullet catching the gypsy high in the breastbone, spinning him clear of the corner of the cabin.

Shotten made a dive for his rifle and came up with it, and then stopped and stared into the maw of Dannifer's Dragoon Colt. Romaine was on the ground, bleeding and kicking and near to dying, and no one really cared enough to look at him.

Dannifer said, "Shotten, you damned near made a fatal mistake there. Let the rifle drop."

Another gypsy appeared around the corner of the cabin and knelt by Romaine; he looked up at Shotten and Dannifer and said, "He is badly wounded."

Shotten didn't even glance at him; he kept looking at Pete Dannifer's .44 pistol and he stood still, his face slack and drained of color. Dannifer said, "Suppose you tell me where the cow is?"

"Lean-to," Shotten said, nodding his head in that direction.

"You walk ahead of me," Dannifer said.

Shotten stepped clear of the cabin and Dannifer kneed his horse forward until the hooves found Shotten's rifle. The stock broke with a snap and the barrel was bent. Shotten watched, his face dark with rage.

"You got no right to ruin a man's property," he said.

"Get the cow."

Shotten put her on a lead rope and Dannifer tied the end to his saddle horn and backed his horse away. At the road he turned and rode back toward the Wilkerson place, leading the cow at a pace just a little faster than she liked to travel.

He figured he'd opened a bag of trouble, but Romaine hadn't given him much choice when he threw the knife. And there wasn't much doubt in Dannifer's mind that the gypsy had stolen the cow, along with the pig and chickens. As he rode along he wondered why they had gone to that much trouble. His knowledge of gypsies was sketchy; the first he'd ever seen were in east Texas, and once they started their stealing, they had been run out. But he'd heard some stories —he really didn't know how true they were—about how gypsies would steal a baby and raise it as their own.

It was something to think about. Wilkerson's wife was due. Maybe they meant to lure Ora Wilkerson away from the place, take the woman and the child she carried. Later they'd kill her and keep the child.

That just might be it, Dannifer thought. It was a terrible thing to think about, but he'd lived through Indian fighting and their cruelty, and he had long ago lost his gentle ideals concerning people.

Wilkerson was relieved to see the cow, and he took her to the lean-to and tied her securely. Then he came back to the cabin. "I see that Shotten milked her," he said.

"The gypsies milked her," Dannifer said. "You've got troubles here, Wilkerson."

The man rubbed his lean face and nodded, his manner grave. "I'm surprised Shotten let you have the cow. He's not a man to give up a thing once he gets his hands on it."

"I know," Dannifer said. He hunkered down by the cabin wall and looked at the timber. "How far to the river?"

"A mile. Why?"

"I'd get out if I were you."

"Leave this? All this work?" Wilkerson shook his head. Then he looked at Dannifer. "What happened at Shotten's place?"

"Tempers let go," Dannifer said. "A knife was thrown. A gun went off."

"I thought I heard a shot. Is Shotten dead?"

"No," Dannifer said. "But a gypsy called Romaine may be before dark. It won't end there, though. We'd better take turns stayin' awake tonight."

He spent his time rubbing down his saddle horse and pack horse, and cleaning and reloading his pistol. In the middle of the afternoon Tammy McCain left the cabin and came to the lean-to. She had a tin plate and a cup of coffee.

"Warmed-over stew," she said. "I'll cook this evening."

"I'm easily satisfied," Dannifer said. "How's Wilkerson's wife?"

"She's startin' labor," Tammy said. "The doctor ought to be here. It'll be a long one, and hard for her."

He said, "Can't Wilkerson go?"

"Can you make him?"

Dannifer thought about it, then said, "I can try," and went to the cabin. Tammy went inside and Wilkerson came out. Dannifer unbuckled his pistol belt and handed it to Wilkerson. "Put this on and ride to Salem for the doctor. Take my horse." He saw the hesitation in Wilkerson, and his voice hardened. "Man, I don't mean to argue with you about this thing. The girl just can't handle it alone."

"Will you stay?" Wilkerson asked.

"I'm here now. I'll be here when you get back. And don't spare the horse. Wear him out gettin' there. Leave him in the livery and come back with the doctor. And keep your damned eyes open and your hand on that pistol." He took the man by the shoulder and turned him to the lean-to, giving him another push. "I've got another in my saddlebag."

Dannifer started with Wilkerson to the lean-to, and every time the man hesitated or started to argue, Dannifer gave him a shove to keep him moving. Finally Wilkerson mounted, and he said, "You get your way, don't you?"

"When I have to," Dannifer said. "Watch out for the gypsies. Don't let them stop you. Until you get to the McCain place, ride with the pistol in hand and keep it cocked."

"I've never shot a man," Wilkerson said. Then he wheeled the horse and rode out of the yard, galloping down the road.

Pete Dannifer went back to the cabin and stopped by the door. Tammy McCain came out.

"You did that without much trouble," she said. "He would never have left me alone with her."

"No man would," Dannifer said. He added, "I don't suppose he has any tobacco. I ran out some weeks ago."

She shook her head. "Neither chewin' nor smokin'. He don't have any whiskey either."

"It's no time for a man to drink whiskey," he said. "I'll sleep until dark, 'cause I want to be up and about tonight."

She frowned. "Is there going to be trouble?" She put her hand on his arm.

He told her briefly what had happened at Shotten's place. She didn't grow pale or clasp her hands together or turn into a silly woman at all. Quite calmly she said, "I'll keep Wilkerson's rifle handy."

"I have a double shotgun," he said. "Better take that too. Are you afraid?"

"Yes, but it won't set me to cryin' about it."

He looked at her because he liked to look at her; then he laughed and said, "I do think I'd stop to call on you after all, Tammy."

This pleased her; she smiled and color came into her face. "Would you fight over me too?"

"Would you want me to?"

She thought about it, and shook her head. "No, not you. That's funny, because Neal Shute fought over me and I liked it. But with you I wouldn't like it. Maybe it's because when Neal told me things I really didn't believe him. But if you told me things, I'd believe them. You wouldn't have to prove anything to me."

He had arrived, he knew, at that moment in his life where a woman was more than just something to look at, and it brought him up short. It didn't cause him to hesitate, though. "Tammy, I think you could stop a wandering man's feet from moving. A fella don't roam because he's looking for the rainbow. He moves because there's nothing to hold him."

"You said you liked Oregon."

"I did," Dannifer said. "If you loved a man, Tammy, how long would you keep him dangling?"

"Not long," she said. "I make up my mind, quick."

He wiped a hand across his face. "We're goin' to talk about this some more." He moved close to her, and then he put his arms around her and kissed her and her lips were softer than he had thought. When he drew away, his held breath was a tight pain in the chest. He smiled and said, "What's the use of talk?"

"None at all," she said, and patted his arm. "Get your sleep now. I've got to stay with Mrs. Wilkerson."

"Anything I can do—"

"No, nothing," she said.

In the lean-to he settled on some loose hay and slept for a time; a whistle woke him. The sun was low. He looked out and saw the gypsies on the road, and he picked up his pistol and went to the cabin.

A huge man with long hair and a bright handkerchief

around his head detached himself from the group and came close to the cabin. He was smiling; an earring dangled to his left shoulder.

"I am Passeau, leader of my people," he said, looking at the pistol. "That is a magnificent weapon." His dark eyes met Dannifer's. "Romaine is dying. The bullet can't be taken from him."

"Why tell me?" Dannifer said. "I didn't shoot to wound him, any more than he threw the knife to miss me."

Passeau shrugged his heavy shoulders. "I am sorry about the misunderstanding over the cow. When we found it, it was roaming free." He waved his hand at the people standing in the road. "My people are warm and friendly. Have you no food to offer them? Tobacco? Coffee?"

"About the only thing we have around here," Dannifer said, "is six little bullets. Now, if your friends think they can digest 'em, tell 'em to come on in for their helping."

Spreading his big hands, Passeau said, "The time is not now, my friend. Darkness brings sleep to the eyes. We will wait."

"You do that. We'll be here."

"A lone man and two women?" He laughed softly. "The other rode through. He surprised us. Coming back will not be as easy."

"Fella, by morning you're liable to be dead," Dannifer said. "Move on now. You're not going to get the kid."

Passeau's expression changed briefly, then his smile became a mask and he bowed and left the yard. Dannifer stood there and watched him go. When he turned he found Tammy McCain standing in the doorway with the shotgun. He took it from her and set it inside, then put his arms around her and held her for a moment.

"I heard what you said. They want the baby?" He nodded, and she looked at him, tipping her head back. "Why?"

"To sell him," Dannifer said. "Don't you know a childless couple might give fifty dollars for a baby?" He put his hand on her shoulder for a moment and stepped inside the cabin.

A glance told him how Wilkerson had built, in a hurry, for he had arrived during the summer and had been pressed for shelter before winter. The cabin was one room, with the bed in one corner, table in the center, and fireplace along the west wall.

Mrs. Wilkerson lay in the bed, her face drawn and pale, and Dannifer was shocked to find her so young. He had expected a woman in her mid-twenties, but she seemed to be only about sixteen, certainly no older.

"I've heard your voice," she said softly. "We're grateful." Her breathing was heavy. She was going to have a time of it, and Dannifer was glad he'd made Wilkerson go for the doctor; this wasn't a delivery a young woman should handle by herself.

"You try and get some sleep," Dannifer said. "Everything's goin' to be all right." He reached down and patted her hand and then turned and went outside; Tammy followed him. After he closed the door, she sat down on the stoop.

"I'm afraid for her. She ain't very hippy, to begin with," Tammy said.

He looked at her. "You pretty good at deliverin' babies?"

"I've helped with a few," she said. "But it's goin' to be hard for her. It ain't right to bear children so young."

"That's the trouble with the world," Dannifer said. "A lot in it ain't right." He smiled and looked at the smooth slimness of her hips. "You suppose you'll have the same trouble?"

She was a little shocked, but not much. "Well, I'm not scared to try," she said. "There's beans and potatoes for supper. Hope that satisfies you."

His smile remained. "I told you I was easily satisfied."

"You don't look like the kind to me," she said. And she got up and flounced into the cabin.

Chapter 4

Wilkerson and the doctor left Salem late in the afternoon. The sky was turning muddy, promising more rain. They rode in Doctor Mandeley's buggy, with Dannifer's horse tied on behind. Mandeley drove, keeping the horse at a loose trot, and he kept up a running stream of talk.

"Damn fools, that's what you are. Think you can get along without a doctor. Too tight to spend a few dollars. Think a woman's a cow or something? Wait till the last minute, then hope you're not too late. Never will understand you people. Never will at all." He looked hard at Ora Wilkerson. "Why the hell couldn't you have built closer to town? What's wrong with livin' close to people?"

Mandeley was a small, unkempt man, not a very good doctor, but the only one Salem had. He was a rough, tobacco-chewing man with the milk of human kindness long dried in his breast, and when he went on a call like this, he always collected his fee in advance.

Darkness found them still on the road, and Wilkerson took his big pistol from beneath his coat and held it in his hand.

Mandeley looked at him. "What are you doing that for?"

"There's gypsies near Shotten's place. They've been making trouble."

"Good Lord," Mandeley said, and he reached beneath the seat and brought out a double-barreled sawed-off shotgun. He checked the percussion caps, then held the shotgun in his lap. "If you'd have told me this before we left Salem—"

"You'd never have left at all," Wilkerson said. "We all know you, Doc."

"Mmm," Mandeley said. "That wasn't a compliment."

He drove as rapidly as he could, and after they passed the McCain place both men sharpened their caution.

"I don't expect they'll be this far," Wilkerson said. "McCain may not even know they're in this neck of the woods. If we have trouble, it'll be between my place and Shotten's."

"The man's mad to have gypsies on his place at all," Mandeley said. "I saw them in Georgia once. It took hanging to get rid of them."

"You're the one who's got to get through," Wilkerson said. He reached back and pulled on the lead rope and brought the horse alongside, then left the buggy for the saddle. "I'm going ahead. If trouble starts, you whip the horse and go on through. No matter what, you keep going, you understand?"

"I had no intention of stopping," Mandeley said flatly. "I never thought for a minute that your skin was more important than mine."

Wilkerson said something under his breath and rode on ahead, leading the buggy by twenty yards, and Mandeley had to keep pace or drop dangerously far behind. As they neared the Shotten place, Wilkerson pulled farther away, increasing his speed, and Mandeley cursed him for leaving him exposed like that.

When the gypsies jumped Wilkerson, Mandeley realized what the settler had done. By leaving Mandeley some distance behind, he had lulled the gypsies into thinking that both men were mounted on his own horse, and in the darkness they could not tell any different. Immediately Wilkerson began shooting, and wheeling his horse in choppy circles, and this gave Mandeley the cover and confusion he needed to drive on through.

But he had a conscience, and as he passed he fired both barrels of the shotgun at two gypsies who leaped at the rig from the brush beside the road. Whether he killed them or not he didn't know and didn't care, but it was a surprise they hadn't been set for, and it took some of the pressure off Wilkerson, who followed the buggy, emptying the remaining chambers of the pistol as he rode on.

When they got to the Wilkerson place, Pete Dannifer met them. Mandeley got down and rushed inside. Ora Wilkerson slowly fell from his horse, and would have struck the ground if Dannifer hadn't caught him.

There was a gypsy knife in Wilkerson's thigh, and the man cried out when Dannifer pulled it free. Then he helped him to the lean-to. From inside the cabin they could hear Wilkerson's wife crying out in pain; this trailed off when the doctor gave her a strong whiff of ether.

Though Dannifer hated to risk a light in the lean-to, he put a match to a coal-oil lantern and hung it on a nail. Then he tore Wilkerson's pants leg open and looked at the wound. "I'm going to have to do something about that," he said. "It'll be shooting poison up your leg by morning."

"Give me a little tap with the barrel of your pistol then," Wilkerson said. "I don't want to raise a fuss."

"That's about what I had in mind," Dannifer said, and struck his fist solidly against the hinge of Wilkerson's jaw. The man fell back, his head rolling loosely, and Dannifer reached for his powder flask. He triggered a little black powder into the open wound, then put a match to it, turning his head when it flared and stank of seared flesh. Wilkerson jerked, then went still again.

Dannifer hurried to the cabin. He didn't knock, just went in, and wished he hadn't, because he'd never seen a baby born before, let alone one being taken.

He saw some clean cloth, grabbed a piece, and dashed out. Wilkerson came around as Dannifer bandaged the leg, and the settler gasped for breath, so sharp was the pain.

"You'll be all right," Dannifer said, and put out the lantern. "Where's my pistol?"

"Belt," Wilkerson said, and Dannifer fumbled for it. He reloaded it in the dark, and handed it back to Wilkerson. "I'm going around to the side of the cabin. You stay here. We'll have company."

"The doc has a shotgun in his buggy. If you could reload it and bring it to me—"

"I'll take care of it," Dannifer said, and left the lean-to.

He found the shotgun and the bag of shot, and a small leather wheel with percussion caps stuck on the nipples, but there was no powder. Pistol powder, he knew, would be a little fine and deliver quite a kick, but under the circumstances he didn't think Wilkerson would mind. He loaded the shotgun and took it to the lean-to.

"Did the doc hit anything with this?" Dannifer asked.

"He might have. Too many things was happening at once to tell." He shifted position and groaned at the effort. "I killed one. He came out of the dark and stabbed me. The pistol wasn't ten inches from his face when I pulled the trigger." He hesitated for a moment. "I could see it all in the muzzle flash. I'll never forget that."

"You'd better keep your mind on what you're doin'," Dannifer said, and left him.

He would have liked it a lot better if the place had been dark, but Doctor Mandeley needed light and it shone yellow from the two front windows. He would have liked to know what was going on inside. It was taking a long time, and now and then he could hear Mandeley swearing, or snapping an order at Tammy McCain.

Dannifer kept his eyes open, and his ears cocked for the first cry of the baby, but he waited a long time and didn't hear it. Then the lamps were turned down and Tammy came out; she saw him crouched in the shadows by the corner and came to him and began to cry.

In a moment Mandeley came out too; he rolled his sleeves down and slipped into his coat. He spoke very softly. "The baby was turned; I knew I couldn't save it, so I tried to save her. I didn't do that either."

Dannifer said, "Go in and turn the lamps back up."

"What!" Mandeley exclaimed, looking sharply at him.

"Damn it, if Wilkerson learns the truth now, he'll fold up," Dannifer said. "And tonight ain't the night for a man to give up."

"Mmm," Mandeley said. "I never thought of it that way."

"Then you think of it that way," Dannifer said. "And after

you turn the lights up, you take the shotgun and make for the edge of the woods. Take Tammy with you."

"Hell, I couldn't do that," Mandeley said. "I'm here—I'll stay here."

He went back in the cabin and turned the lamps up. When he came out again, he asked, "Where's the best place to wait?"

"About twenty miles from here," Dannifer said. "But since we can't do that, suppose you go to the lean-to with Wilkerson."

"He'll ask me—"

"Then lie to him, you damned fool!" Dannifer said, and went back to his business of studying the blackness of the yard and beyond.

Tammy stayed by him. Finally she spoke in a voice so soft he scarcely heard her. "If Wilkerson had called the doctor sooner—"

"The world's made up of ifs, Tammy. Thinking about it gets you nothing but tears and a runny nose."

"If the gypsies thought the baby was dead—"

"They'd come in anyway," Dannifer said, "'cause they wouldn't believe it. Stop ifing. I had to learn. Two of my brothers were taken by the Comanches. It's been near ten years. They're full-grown bucks now, raidin' and killin' and not knowing the difference, or caring either. A long time ago my pa stopped lookin' and ma quit cryin'."

For a long while they shared no more talk, only the waiting. There was no light, no moon, and finally the rain began to fall—gently at first, then more heavily, but they stayed outside in it, being soaked to the skin. Dannifer could no longer judge the time; he knew it must be late because he felt so sleepy.

Suddenly a noise startled him; it was not much of a sound, but it did not belong in the natural realm of sounds. Before he could figure out what it was, a gun went off by the lean-to; then there was no more shooting, just the grunting of men and the thudding violence of man against man.

He knew what that meant; it was like Indian fighting. "They've been jumped," he said, and he took her hand and went quickly around the cabin. He made for the woods, and when they reached them he stopped for a look back and saw the gypsies going into the cabin.

Dannifer knew what that meant too; they'd be willing to take second best: Tammy McCain. "We've got to reach the river," he said, and they hurried through the woods. The rain was heavy, kicking up a sound of its own, and it covered their movement very well. When they reached the road, Dannifer stopped for a quick look, then darted across, drawing Tammy with him.

The river was a quarter of a mile further through the woods and they had to slow down, for they could not see; even going carefully they both fell more than once. He heard the river before they came to it, heard the movement of it and the sound of the rain on it. They stopped at a cut bank.

"Can you swim?" he asked.

"Some," she said.

"Get that dress off; it'll just drag you down," he said, and sat down and pulled off his boots. When he stood up to strip off his leather shirt he saw her still standing there; she hadn't moved. Dannifer reached out and ripped her dress down the front, jerked at it until it fell around her feet. Then he peeled off his shirt and dropped it, and pushed her into the water, diving in after her.

She was splashing and trying to stay afloat when he reached her, and he hooked an arm around her and started downstream, swimming easily, with long, steady strokes.

Between breaths he said, "Relax, relax—I'll tow you along."

They drifted and swam for what he judged to be about a mile, then he started in toward the near bank. But he couldn't quite reach it, for the current was very strong and kept towing him out, moving them along. He could have risked all his strength and tried to make the bank, but he felt that if he failed in such an attempt they might both drown. He didn't like that idea at all.

It was a fast river, with considerable fall to it, and he figured they'd run into rapids soon enough and he would need help then. Their best chance would be a deadfall that they could cling to and save their strength. He started to ease toward the bank again, not fighting the current, just stubbornly working that way as the river carried them along.

A floating branch rapped against his head so suddenly that he nearly let go of Tammy; he grabbed with his free hand and realized that he had hold of the snag end of a good-sized log. With some effort he got her against the log, got her holding on, and he kept her between the log and himself, an arm on each side of her so she wouldn't let go and go down.

The rain was furious now, raising a roar on the river that nearly drowned out his voice.

"Kind of moist out, ain't it?"

She heard him and turned her head to look at him. He put his mouth on hers and kissed her, holding her that way longer than was proper, and he could feel her body against his, feel a rising response in her. For a moment he brought her mind away from the danger of the river, and the danger behind them.

It was a good moment, but it ended; and the sound of the river grew stronger, more violent, like thunder in the distance; he knew they were coming to the hard part, the rapids. He boosted her up on the bole of the log and shouted for her to hold on. She heard the mounting roar and knew what it was, and he was glad that he could not see her face, glad that she could not see his, and the fear there.

The thought of losing her was a torment to him. He reached down and unbuckled his pistol belt and let the gun and shot pouch and powder horn slide off, to be lost in the river. This hurt, for the pistol was precious to him; a year of saving had gone into the buying of the pair. Now they were gone, but he put that aside and looped the belt around her wrist, holding the free end in his hand.

His grip was so tight that it hurt, but he didn't lessen it.

The log took a sickening plunge, one end rising out of the water, then it rolled and started to move faster. The water foamed around them, and it was just a matter of hanging on and hoping your brains didn't get splattered on a rock. He put an arm around her, holding on with his fingers in the rough bark as though he meant to shield her with his own body. He felt her hand on his, tightly, her fingernails digging into him, but there was no pain at all.

He felt the log hit a rock, jarring them; then it rolled, broke free, and plunged on.

That's just the first, he thought, then there wasn't time to think, or the need of it.

Chapter 5

His name was Tanan Two Bear, and it was the third name he had taken in his life. The first was given when he reached manhood many years before; the second when he killed his first enemy. The third was taken when he led his people.

Tanan Two Bear was a tall Indian, gray of locks but still lean in the flanks; old in wisdom, yet young enough to hunt with the strongest of his tribe.

The hunting had not been good this year, for the snow had come early and the strong game had already left the high reaches of the mountains. Tanan Two Bear was disappointed, but not empty-handed, though he had wanted to return to his village with each man heavy with meat. It was not to be, so he sent the bulk of his braves back with the game, and with three others left the high reaches for a swing through the valley.

There was a possibility that he might find game there, but he did not care whether he did or not. Before the settlers came the valley had been home to Tanan Two Bear, and he sometimes went back, to see how they had destroyed the land with their cabins and fields and roads slashing through the woods.

In his old breast there was still a strong hatred for the white man, but he had fought them and lost, and now his people were small in number and they would never fight again, or even be strong again, so the hatred was a banked fire that would smoke until his death, but it would never flare up again.

Tanan Two Bear and his three braves camped in the woods and the rain fell heavily and made a miserable night of it. In the first light of morning they moved across the valley. The rain continued in a drizzle and the sky was low and gray. The land was a flat green basin, but the mountains were completely blotted out.

Chance brought them near the Wilkerson place. Tanan Two Bear saw no smoke coming from the cabin chimney, and this puzzled him, for the weather was chilly and there would always be a cook fire. He decided to have a closer look, and as he drew near the place he heard the milk cow complaining about a full udder. This roused his suspicions and he grew bolder; he waved his braves to scatter, and they approached the place from three sides.

One of the braves found the bodies of Wilkerson and Mandeley by the lean-to, and Tanan Two Bear rushed over for a look. There were some prints in the yard, but the rain had done quite a good job of erasing them. Two braves made a quick tour away from the lean-to and came back.

Tanan Two Bear held up four fingers, indicating the number who had attacked the two men. Then he went to the cabin and cautiously pushed open the door with the muzzle of his old trade musket. Inside he found the dead woman and the baby, and he liked none of this. He went outside again and had a conference with his braves.

The story was partially written in the grass, for it had been wet when trampled and held impressions well. The four had killed the two men; six had attacked the cabin. But the woman and child had died of natural causes; Tanan Two Bear found small comfort in this.

But there was opportunity too. The dead men had no further use for weapons or for the horses; Tanan Two Bear ordered them caught up and brought along, and they began to follow the trail to the river; the tracks through the grass were still visible to one trained in following the slightest sign.

One of the braves found Tammy McCain's dress and brought it to Tanan Two Bear, who could not make much of it. He examined it, then gave it back to the brave who had found it. He was beginning to feel the presence of bad medicine, and within him there was a growing haste to be gone from this place. After all, he had two horses and a shotgun and a heavy pistol; he was not a man to let his greed get the best of him.

Still it was their Indian way to loop back past the cabin just to see if there was anything they'd missed. One of the braves took a liking to the doctor's hat and exchanged it for his own headband; then Tanan Two Bear waved them on and they made good time away from Wilkerson's place.

Angus McCain nursed a growing worry most of the day, and in the early afternoon he called his son in from the field and told him to go to the rise a mile to the south and watch for Wilkerson's smoke.

"Stay there until daylight is gone, if you have to," McCain said.

After the boy left, McCain worked near the barn; he wanted to be close to the house. Muley Shotten came by in his wagon, bound for Salem, and he waved at McCain, who waved back. Then Muley passed on down the road.

An hour later, a horseman turned in and came to the barn, where he flung off. Neal Shute looked at his mud-splattered horse, then bent and picked up some straw and cleaned his boots. He was a dark young man with a serious manner, and the muscle to back his opinions.

He looked to the house as though he expected someone to run out to greet him, but Angus McCain said, "She ain't here, Neal."

This seemed to anger the young man. "Then where the thunder is she?"

"Wilkerson's place," McCain said. "Baby time. Mrs. Wilkerson needed a woman."

"Your wife's a woman," Shute said, then closed his mouth, realizing that he was telling another man how to run his business. He took out a cigar and lit it, and as an afterthought offered one to McCain, who started to take it, then shook his head.

"Well, damned if I'm going to ride to Wilkerson's," Shute said. "I'll stay the night, and till noon tomorrow. If she ain't back then, she can invite me special the next time."

"How's business in Salem?" McCain asked.

"Thriving," Shute said. "I may enlarge the store. Some families came down from Portland; they mean to settle in the Willamette." He puffed his cigar and rocked back on his heels. "I'm a member of the town council now. Some of my friends think I ought to run for a higher office once we become a state of the union." He looked at McCain as though hoping to get a promise of support, or his vote, but McCain's Scotch reticence held him silent; there was no encouragement in his expression at all.

Shute continued to puff on his cigar, and frowned. "Building up for more rain."

"Appears that way," McCain said.

There was silence while Shute smoked. Then he said, "I saw Muley Shotten on the road with a load of potatoes. I bought 'em on the spot." He looked at McCain as though he invited comment, but McCain said nothing. Finally Shute said, "I tried to buy his cats too, but he wouldn't sell. I offered the damned idiot a dollar apiece too."

"What cats?" McCain asked.

"He had three cats, that's all. What's so odd about that?"

"The old man don't cotton to animals," McCain said. "Muley brought home a pup last year and the old man killed it. Thought there was going to be trouble over that, but it blew over." He glanced at Neal Shute. "What did you want the cats for?"

"Thought we might have a little sport," Shute said. "Salem needs a little manly game now and then. I know a man who's got a feisty dog. It occurred to me that if we had a dog-and-cat fight, we might draw a crowd."

"At a dollar a head?" McCain asked.

"Well, I was thinking more of a dollar and a half," Shute said. "I know fifty men who'd pay that to see whether a dog lost an eye before he killed a cat."

McCain took a deep beath and held it until his face turned red. He turned and put his hands on the upper rail of the fence and stood that way for several minutes, gripping it as though he were in danger of falling.

Shute looked around, commenting, "I see a constant improvement in the place, Angus. One of these days when you've gone to your reward, it'll be a worthy monument to leave to your son-in-law."

"Aye," McCain said, "which makes picking the son-in-law a careful bit of business." He let go of the fence rail and turned back to Shute. "My daughter's made no promise to you?"

"No," Shute said, showing his irritation. "Can't the girl make up her mind?"

"I'll do my best to encourage her to make up her mind," Angus McCain said.

Neal Shute's manner brightened and he teetered on his heels again, the cigar jauntily upthrust from between his teeth. McCain almost smiled at the man's conceit and knew he wouldn't have to enlarge on that statement; Shute naturally assumed that McCain would plead for him.

Now and then McCain turned his head and stared toward the south pasture and the forest beyond. This attracted Shute's attention; he turned and looked too, then he asked, "Are you worried about something?"

"I told her to have Wilkerson send up smoke when she got there," McCain said. "I've not seen any."

"She might have forgot."

He shook his head. "Tammy knows it's important. I've sent the boy to the far rise to watch." He looked at the dull sky. "I hope the rain holds off. I'd hate to have to go to Wilkerson's tonight."

"I met Wilkerson on the town road," Shute said.

McCain stared at him. "You must have been mistaken, Shute."

"No mistake. He was in a hell-bent hurry. Nearly crowded me off the road in his rush to get by." He looked at the diminishing stub of his cigar. "Didn't you see him pass?"

McCain shook his head. "Come to the house, Shute. Make no mention of this to my wife. She worries too much as it is, and if she knew Tammy was alone—"

He let the rest trail off. Shute nodded, and went with him to the cabin. Mrs. McCain met them at the door. "I've got fresh coffee ready to pour. You're looking well, Neal."

"Feeling well," he said, taking off his hat and stepping inside. "My, this is indeed a homey place. It's the woman, I always say." He sat down at the table while McCain went to the mantel for his pipe and tobacco. "I brought you something from the store," Neal said. "I'll go fetch it for you."

He went out to his saddlebag, and Mrs. McCain said, "Now there's a nice man, Angus. A real nice man. It pleases me so to think he's taken with our Tammy."

"Aye," McCain said quietly. "When I think of him as a son-in-law I ask myself what I've done to deserve him."

Shute came back with an oilcloth-wrapped bundle. He laid it on the table and unwrapped it. There was some brightly colored yard goods and a heavy winter blanket.

"My," Mrs. McCain said, "ain't they grand!"

"Just some samples of stock from my store," Shute said. "On the last boatload I bought there were glass plates and fine copper pots from the east coast. Got a full stock of farm implements now, including the new John Deere plows. I'd be glad to hold some of these things for you, Angus, if you'd give me some idea when you were coming to town."

"We'll be in soon," McCain said, "but don't put yourself out for us."

"It's no trouble," Neal Shute said, smiling. "Why, it's just putting the best aside for the family." He looked at Mrs. McCain. "When I was wrapping the blanket and cloth, I thought: *This is for Mother McCain.*"

"That was sweet of you, Neal."

Angus McCain suddenly found his pipe not drawing well and gave it his best attention. Neal Shute said, "I would have brought something for Tammy, but I didn't want to be forward."

"She's getting you, Neal," McCain said. "That's enough for any girl."

For a moment, Shute sat there wondering about that, then he smiled and took it exactly the way McCain knew he would take it.

"It's a pity Tammy isn't here," Mrs. McCain said. "In the morning you might like to ride over to Wilkerson's."

"The thought had occurred to me," Shute said. "But it's building up to rain. Best to wait till it's over. The road's bad when it's muddy."

McCain said nothing; he was turning over in his mind some alternatives and liking none of them. If he went tonight —he was sure he could think of a pretense that would fool his wife—he'd have to go alone, because Shute wouldn't pass up a warm bed for a night ride. And it would mean a miserable trip in the rain; the look of the sky forecast a real gully-buster, and McCain was pretty good at guessing the weather. Morning might be soon enough, or too late; it was a question that would have to wait for an answer.

Quincy came back just after dark—a bit late for supper, and his mother scolded him. The boy held his tongue, but when she turned away, he looked at his father and shook his head, then went on eating.

There had been no smoke, and McCain knew why; that fool Wilkerson had gone to town, probably to get drunk. A slow anger built in McCain's mind, and he decided to knock Wilkerson down in the morning, just to teach the man a lesson. Wilkerson was considered a new man to the valley and to the Territory; because of this he didn't take his responsibilities seriously enough, didn't think ahead.

The rain came, as McCain knew it would, and he spent a poor night, sleeping in fits and waking, impatiently waiting for the dawn. It came, and he hurried through breakfast, got his rifle and went to the barn for his horse. Shute was in no hurry, but McCain edged him along.

Quincy rode double with his father, and he carried a shotgun. Neal Shute stayed a little distance behind so he wouldn't be splashed so badly by the mud. The road was a mass of mire, and the drizzle that kept up through the morning didn't help anything either.

Shute wanted to stop at the Shotten place, and although McCain was against the delay he gave in; they found the place abandoned. Shotten's fireplace was cold; the man was gone.

"I don't like this at all," McCain said and mounted up, and they went on to Wilkerson's. When they drew near the place, McCain saw Doctor Mandeley's buggy. It was an alarm bell in his mind, for there was no sign of smoke from the chimney, no sign of movement at all around the place.

He dismounted in the yard, then he saw Wilkerson by the lean-to and ran over, his feet slipping in the mud. The man was cold and stiff. Then he saw Mandeley's body against the wall, frozen in a sitting position.

"Inside!" McCain said, and ran for the cabin.

He flung the door open and stopped, his heart throbbing in his chest. Shute crowded in behind him, then thrust past and looked at the woman and baby. When Quincy tried to see, McCain pushed him back and turned outside, feeling sick in the stomach.

Shute came out then and stood there, rain running off the brim of his hat. He said, "Injuns," and it was what McCain was thinking too.

But it was something a man had to prove to himself; he had to do more than just think it. They went back to the lean-to and looked around. Quincy found the headband, and it was all they needed to make their conclusions.

Neal Shute said, "The way I see it, McCain, they hit sometime in the night. Wilkerson and Mandeley were in the lean-to and were killed first. The woman must have died of fright. The baby—" He shrugged. "A newborn's hold on life is mighty slim as it is. Who knows?"

"Tammy," McCain said. "They must have taken her."

Shute nodded, his face like thunder. "I'll ride to Salem. Let me take your horse; it's fresher. I'll bring back men, maybe twenty. You wait here, McCain. We might be able to pick up a trail."

After Shute had gone, Angus McCain and Quincy went back to the lean-to and got shovels. McCain set the boy to digging a grave behind the cabin while he went inside the cabin, where Wilkerson kept his hand tools. He tore apart the table and bed and all the shelving to get boards for the coffin. After it was made, he took the woman and the baby, wrapped them in a blanket, and put them in the coffin together. Only after he had nailed the lid on did he call the boy, and they carried the box to the grave.

"I don't know whether Wilkerson kept a Bible or not," Angus McCain said. "Leastways I'm of no mind to hunt for it."

He took off his soggy hat and the boy did the same. "Lord, we commend into Thy keeping this poor woman and infant too young to know Thy name. Forgive any sins she might have had and take them into Thy fold. Amen." He clapped his hat back on and they lowered the box and together shoveled dirt over it, patting the mound round and even before putting their tools aside and going to the cabin.

McCain built a roaring fire and stripped to his wet underwear and steamed himself dry. The boy found some towels and rubbed himself until his skin was red, and stood naked before the fire until the heat drove the circulation back into his wet and chilled body.

Finally Quincy said, "Ain't we goin' to bury Mr. Wilkerson and the doctor, pa?"

"I want the others to see 'em," McCain said bleakly. "They'll be here in the morning. There's nothin' to do but wait."

"The Indians got Tammy, huh, pa?"

"I fear they did." McCain spoke quietly. "But she's alive. We must get to her soon, though. There's no tellin' what kind of devilment they will do to her." He clamped his lips together. "When you're dried off, I want you to go back home. Stay with your mother. Tell her what's happened, but soften it, boy. Keep her spirits up if you can. Tell her to pray."

"All right, pa," Quincy said. "But can I come back in the mornin'?"

Angus McCain shook his head. "When we find the Injun camp, there'll be some killing, more than likely. There's no need to be a part of that at your age. You stay with your mother."

The boy left an hour later, afoot, dog-trotting as best he could down the muddy road, and McCain watched him until he was out of sight. He felt a twinge of guilt for leaving Wilkerson and Mandeley stiff and cold in the drizzling rain, but he knew men, knew they would want to look at the gruesome dead in order to get their dander up properly.

It was too bad about Wilkerson, but the real tragedy was losing the doctor; others would die before another could be brought in. He'd have to remind Shute and the other men of this when it came time to deal with the Indians.

McCain had no thought but to bring the guilty ones to Salem for trial; he hoped he could carry out this intention. It wouldn't be easy, he knew, with Neal Shute having his say.

Then, too, he was counting on finding Tammy. If he failed to find her, or if she was dead—McCain couldn't think beyond that point. He didn't want to think beyond it.

Chapter 6

Pete Dannifer felt cold. One by one, his senses came back to him and he opened his eyes. He was flat on his back on a stretch of beach and the rain was falling gently; when he tried to move it felt as if all his muscles had been torn loose. Then he jerked his body erect, ignoring the pain, thinking of Tammy McCain. He saw the log ten yards away, and he saw Tammy half under it, her legs pinned there. Whether she was alive or dead he had no way of knowing. He didn't even know how they had ridden out the rapids, for it was all a dull nightmare somewhere back in a corner of his mind, shoved there, he supposed, because it was too horrible to remember.

His shirt was in tatters and one leg of his leather pants was ripped open down the outside seam. Getting to his feet was more of a chore than he thought it would be, but he was driven by desperation. He could scarcely believe that he had no broken bones, for he remembered hitting some rocks violently; it didn't matter now.

He found a strong branch and, using this as a peavey, he ran his hand over her legs to see if there were any fractures, but there weren't; the soft sandy loam of the beach had absorbed the weight of the deadfall, pressing her legs down, cushioning her, saving her from injury. She had a good-sized welt on her temple and he supposed this was what had knocked her out.

Dannifer looked around to see what could serve as shelter, but he saw nothing on their side of the river save timber and brush, all rain-soaked. What they needed was overhead shelter and a fire. Ahead the river made a sharp turn, and he realized that factor alone had deposited them on this beach. The strong current had shoved them onto it instead of taking them around the bend. On the other side of the river fairly sheer bluffs came to the water's edge, and from where he stood he thought he could see overhangs, or caves carved out by the river's erosion.

There was his shelter, but getting across was going to be more of a problem than he was capable of solving. The current was swift but the water was reasonably calm, and a strong swimmer could have made it, providing he was fresh. Dannifer was beat and weak, and he knew that if he entered the water he'd drown.

So he ruled out crossing and turned his thoughts to the timber and brushy country behind him. He had no knife or gun, and he searched his pocket to see if his tin of matches was still there. He found them after a moment of searching and opened the tin. Long ago he had learned to dip the matches in wax to keep them dry, and he felt that an all-night soaking in the river hadn't hurt them any.

He left Tammy and walked to the edge of the woods and somewhat beyond, until he found a spot beneath some large trees that would serve as a shelter. At a nearby deadfall he kicked at the rotten wood until some of the dry center was exposed, and with this he made his fire, starting it small and building it gradually until it put out a good heat. He banked one side high with wet pieces of wood and they acted as a heat deflector. Then he went back to the beach for Tammy and found that he was barely able to lift her. Staggering, he carried her, almost falling several times, and put her down near the fire. What clothes she had on did her little good and he was sorry now he had left her dress on the bank. Her chemise was in tatters and he could see the welts and contusions on her shoulders and thighs, and she needed something to cover her for warmth, but there was nothing.

Dannifer found two forked pieces of wood and he managed to plant them upright in the ground near the fire. Another pole served as a crosspiece and then he laid branches crudely until the slanting roof was complete. To make it as weather-tight as possible, he dug up the mossy earth with his hands and laid it in thick cakes on the slanting roof. He worked for a couple of hours before he was satisfied with the job, and now and then he turned Tammy around so that she warmed both sides. He tended the fire too while he worked, and always gathered more wood than he needed at the moment, for he was stocking up for the long night ahead. He had no way of knowing the time; the sky was a dull gray and he could not tell whether it was morning or afternoon.

Dannifer piled more pieces of wood around the fire, making a heat shield on three sides and he found that this effectively threw the heat into the lean-to.

He sat down near the fire, close to Tammy, and he reached out and felt her chemise and found it warm and nearly dry. The moss roof was keeping the rain out and the ground near the fire was steaming. In another hour it would be dry.

Dannifer did not know how long he sat there, but he caught himself dozing several times and brought himself awake with a snap. Once he found that the fire was down and hurriedly built it up again. To keep awake, he went in search of more wood and brought three armloads back to the fire.

Tammy groaned, and when he touched her she opened her eyes and looked at him a moment before recognition came. Then she tried to speak, and her lips moved but no words came out. She tried again and said, "Are you—all right?"

He stroked her forehead, brushing the hair back from her face. "You're the one who worried me," Pete Dannifer said. "When I woke up, we were both on a small beach by a bend in the river. Lord knows how we got there." He looked around the woods. "I don't have any idea where we are. Do you?"

She shook her head and tried to sit up, but groaned and sagged back. "I'm not ready for that," she said. "My head's fit to bust open." She raised a hand to her temple, then winced and pulled it away. "I must have taken a real clout."

"Well, we're out of the river anyway," Dannifer said. "But not out of trouble. Night's comin' on and we need more shelter than this."

"The fire feels good," she said, and closed her eyes. He waited a moment for her to say more, then he put his hand on her cheek and realized that she was already asleep. That's good, he thought, and stretched out beside her. He put his arms around her and closed his eyes, meaning to rest this way for just a moment, but when he tried to open them, he found it difficult, impossible, and he surrendered.

The chill brought him awake, fitfully, resentfully, and he saw that the fire was way down. The day was gone too, and he groped for wood and blew the fire into life. He was sorry now that he had slept at all, for he did not know how long it had been dark. He'd lost a day, and now he was going to lose track of the night too. Tammy still slept and he was glad of that; she'd need all her strength if they were going to get out of this one. The trouble with being in this kind of a fix was that though there was always the possibility of a settler living only a few miles away you never knew it, and if you went looking you wore yourself out and died anyway.

Hunger was a pain in Dannifer's stomach. By dawn it would be a gnawing, a cramp that would make him weak. Without a gun he was pretty helpless. He thought of all the game he had trapped as a boy, and then he had bought a gun and lost the knack completely. A man, he decided, was a little too dependent on his firearms. He didn't even have a knife; that had been on his pistol belt that he had let go right after he'd entered the river.

Dannifer thought of being able to fish, but he had nothing to make into a hook; or a line to fasten it to. He sat with his head in his hands, trying to think of something, but nothing came to him.

So he spent the night tending the fire, sleeping a little and waking to worry and to put more wood on the fire. For long periods Tammy didn't stir; then she would groan and roll over and he'd edge her closer to the fire so she wouldn't get cold in her sleep.

The rain stopped during the night, and when dawn came Dannifer saw that they were going to have sunshine; he thought it was a most welcome change and his spirits brightened considerably. It would mean that he could let the fire go out during the day and spend the time on their immediate problems: food and better cover.

When it was fully daylight he walked back to the small stretch of beach and studied the river and the surrounding land. He walked as far upstream as he could; the thicker brush stopped him, for he didn't see any advantage in beating his way through it. While he stood there he caught a bit of movement upstream and crouched down for a better look. A canoe was working down, a lone man back-paddling so he could carefully scan both banks. Dannifer studied him, and from the bright-colored shirt he knew it was one of the gypsies looking for them. They had probably portaged around the rapids, camped farther upstream, and sent this man down for a look.

Dannifer knew that he would see the tracks on the beach

because the rain then hadn't been hard enough to wipe them out. And he'd been careless, making no real attempt to erase them at all.

Without weapons, Dannifer didn't want to meet the gypsy on the beach. I'll have to get him in the water, Dannifer thought, and eased himself into the river; he felt the current tug at him, but he stayed close to shore, near the overhanging brush where he could stay out of sight. The man came on, back-paddling carefully, and he warped his way out of mid-stream and eased toward the beach. Dannifer took a big breath and went under, swimming to meet the canoe.

The water was so muddy that he could not see, and when he surfaced he scraped his forehead against the side of the canoe. The gypsy stared, startled, but recovered quickly and swung his rifle. Dannifer grabbed the barrel and jerked, bracing his knees against the side of the canoe. He never figured out whether it was this tug, or his weight acting as a fulcrum, that upset the canoe, but it went over quickly, spilling the gypsy. Dannifer knew that the man would be using his knife, and he grabbed an arm; the blade cut him slightly and he knew that he'd been lucky, and he got the weapon hand. He felt the man's head against his leg and realized that the gypsy was upside down in the water; Dannifer clamped his throat in a leg scissors and put on all the pressure he had. The man struggled wildly with an insane strength, but Dannifer's was just as intense; this was the only chance he was going to get, and if he failed he was a dead man. And Tammy would be dead too.

They did not surface and Dannifer's lungs felt as if they were going to burst, but he kept clinging to the man, kept choking the life out of him with his legs, and at last the gypsy grew still. Dannifer surfaced for air; he towed the man to the beach and left him there, then swam for the drifting canoe. He caught it before the stronger midstream current took it out of reach, and brought it to the beach.

The gypsy was dead, and Dannifer stripped his clothes off. He found another knife sheathed under the shirt, and a shot pouch and cap box. He had no idea what else the gypsy had been carrying in the canoe, but he went back in the water and dived to the river bottom until he found the bundle and rifle.

He couldn't leave the gypsy on the beach, so he towed him out and let him go; the man sank immediately. Dannifer put everything in the canoe and brushed out all sign of his tracks.

In two trips he carried the gun and the clothes and bundle back to his lean-to, and went through the things carefully.

The gypsy had two blankets and a coat in the bundle, along with a package of food in an oilskin wrapper. There was a tin pot, some coffee, and dried meat and bread, but water had gotten to the bread and Dannifer put it aside to dry out. The gypsy's pants and his shirt, Dannifer figured, he'd give to Tammy; he slipped them on her and it embarrassed him a little to do this, but he did it anyway. The man's belt could be shortened for her; he kept the coat for himself. The blankets were soaked, so he spread them to dry. Then he put on a pot of coffee while he cut up some of the meat.

The smell of the coffee must have penetrated her mind even as she slept, for she stirred, then sniffed and opened her eyes. She looked at him and at the fire and the tin pot beginning to boil.

"I'm dreaming," she said. Then she discovered the clothes on her and sat up. "I'm not dreaming, am I?"

"No," Dannifer said. He hooked the coffee from the edge of the fire and set it aside to cool a bit while he cooked the meat on some sticks he'd sharpened. "One of the gypsies came along in a canoe," he said. "It turned out that he couldn't swim too well."

She said nothing for a moment, then lifted the tin of coffee and sipped, drawing in her breath sharply because it was so hot. "That's better than I've ever tasted. The meat smells good too."

"We'll leave when the sun's high," Pete Dannifer said. "I managed to catch the canoe before it drifted away."

Tammy McCain studied him carefully. "Pete, you're a man who can manage about anything, can't you?"

"Be nice if that was so," he said. "But the truth is, I make about one big mistake a mile. When that gypsy don't report back to camp, the river will be swarming with 'em and I want a head start. A good fast head start."

He ate some meat, and then said, "First thing we've got to do is find out where the blazes we are, and then send word back to your folks that you made it out all right. Your ma and pa must be sick about now, especially if anyone's discovered what happened at Wilkerson's place. You think there's much chance of that?"

"Pa told me to have Wilkerson send up smoke when I got there," Tammy said. "I forgot it, Pete. Plumb forgot it."

"It may be lucky you did," Dannifer said. "If your pa's the frettin' kind he likely went over for a look-see."

He took the tin of coffee when she handed it to him and drank thirstily. "Second to a razor, that's about as good a thing as I can think of," he said. He drank some more, then put the pot down. "Soon as I get some place where I can buy a gun and a horse, I'm goin' back and have a serious talk with Muley Shotten's pa."

She reached out and took his hand. "Pete, there's men who'll take care of Dan Shotten. I'd like to think you had somethin' more important to do." She looked at the lean-to and smiled. "First off, you might take a piece of land and put up a decent roof over my head and get me a decent bed."

"Ain't you rushin' things?"

She shook her head. "Ma's not goin' to understand my bein' alone with a man. I don't think pa'll understand it much better. And there's Neal Shute; he's not going to understand it at all."

"Who's he, anyway?"

"He asked for my hand," Tammy said. "I didn't say yes and I didn't jerk it away either, and Neal Shute's the kind of a man who'll take that kind of answer for yes." She seemed very serious, almost worried. "You'll have some settlin' to do with Neal, I'm sorry to say."

"I'll do that when it's time," Dannifer said solemnly. "But for now I've got bigger worries."

Chapter 7

In an hour, Pete Dannifer had erased all sign of the lean-to and the fire. He went to the beach and got the canoe out of the brush, loaded it, put Tammy in the bow, and pushed off, heading downriver. He wasn't very experienced with a canoe and he handled the paddle clumsily, working himself into a sweat before he got the hang of it.

Before the day was through, Dannifer ran some white water, but he managed to keep the canoe right side up and felt pretty good about the fact that he hadn't stove a hole in it. Toward evening he started looking for a likely campsite, and settled for an open glen on the west bank. He beached the canoe, hid it well, then led the way into the timber, back from the river far enough so that their fire wouldn't be seen. This was rough country, and rocky, and he found a shallow cave, a bit small to stand in, but just right for sleeping. He built a fire and banked it with wood so that it threw heat and light into the cave; Tammy made the coffee and cut up the rest of the meat for a stew. Some of the bread could be saved by cutting away the mold.

Dannifer was inclined to long periods of silence, but finally he said, "Today did you see any stretch of the river that you recognized?"

"No," Tammy said. "It's all strange to me. But I don't think there's a town between Salem and Oregon City. And we're a far piece past Salem. I'm sure of that."

"Is the Oregon City road on this bank or the other?"

She thought a moment. "I've only been there twice. Let's see, goin' toward Oregon City the river's on the left. It'd be on the other side."

"In the morning I'm cuttin' across country until we run into the road," Dannifer said. "That way we stand a chance of comin' onto some place, or meetin' someone traveling the road. We might spend another three or four days on the river the rate we're going."

"Whatever you want, Pete," Tammy said.

"It's going to be tougher traveling on foot, but I don't see any other way. If you're stiff and bruised up—"

"I'll make out," she said. "The coffee's ready."

"And I'm ready for the coffee," he said, and took the tin pot. It burned his fingers and he put it down and blew on them and waved them, then laughed and knelt on all fours to take the first sip. "That's better coffee than I can make," he said.

"Well now, I expect it is," Tammy said. "You can't do everything the best."

For Angus McCain, the waiting was the most difficult part of it, but he could do nothing but wait. Neal Shute came back and he had his twenty men, plus a couple extra; they dismounted in the yard and looked at the dead men as though they had to see them with their own eyes before they could get properly angry.

Shute smoked one of his cigars and spoke to McCain. "I believe it would be foolish to waste any more time here."

"I've thought that for the last seven hours," McCain said. "Did you bring provisions? I took none when I left my place."

"We've enough," Shute said, and went to his horse. He mounted and waited, then got down again. "I suppose we ought to bury 'em," he said, and motioned for two of the men to start the grave digging.

"That's been done," McCain said. "Say somethin' over 'em if you want, but we leave in five minutes."

"It can be done quicker than that," Shute said.

Someone went into the cabin and brought out two blankets and the dead men were wrapped in them and placed in the grave McCain had dug behind the lean-to. Shute stood there looking around, waiting for a volunteer to say something reverent. Finally McCain said, "If nobody can think of anything good about these men, I can."

He glanced about. Some of these men he knew; mostly they were strangers and he wondered where Neal Shute had collected them. Two men were still shoveling dirt when McCain spoke. "Lord, we give unto Your keeping these two souls. Like all of us, their sins were foolish and mostly needless, and they were as sorry for 'em as we all are of ours. We ask You to remember this when the score is added and—"

"That's enough to get anyone through," Shute said brusquely. "Throw on a couple more scoops, Abe, and let's get out of here." He turned and went around the lean-to and McCain stood there a moment as though he meant to say more. Then he clamped his hat on his head and followed Shute.

When he came up to him he said, "These men are strangers to me, 'ceptin' a few."

Shute was checking the cinch on his saddle and he looked up quickly at McCain. "What did you want on this party? Friends?" He laughed shortly. "McCain, you're a good man, and maybe now that's a drawback. I offered two dollars a day and some excitement, and got the kind of men that offer appeals to. Suppose you mount up."

"You're in charge here?"

"As sure as God made green apples," Shute said, and swung up.

They left Wilkerson's place and took a northerly direction,

McCain riding behind Neal Shute. The others strung out behind, except for two bearded men who went on ahead and seemed to scout the trail. They rode this way for better than three hours; then one of the scouts wheeled and rode back to Shute. He chewed tobacco, and the untidy habit immediately set McCain against him. And, too, he didn't like the cut of the man, or of any of them; the familiar stamp of hard work wasn't on any of them. Of hard living, yes, but not hard work. There wasn't a farmer among them, or a timber man. They were all trappers and meat hunters, and likely thieves and worse; all McCain's strong prejudices were aroused by them and he wondered if it would be safe to close his eyes and sleep.

None of this seemed to bother Neal Shute, who said, "What is it, Abe?"

"Been some Injuns this way recent like," Abe said. "They had horses. Seen dung twice now. Was I to offer an opinion, I'd say they was headin' toward their camp somewheres around Oregon City. They usually gather at that end of the woods this time of the year."

"Let's not waste any time then," Shute said. He thought a moment. "Likely the horses taken from Wilkerson's. Can you tell how many?"

"Four," Abe said.

Shute frowned. "Wilkerson had one and Mandeley had one. Where'd the other two come from?"

Abe shrugged and rode back to join his friend who waited fifty yards ahead. When they moved out, Shute motioned the rest of them on. McCain expected Shute to turn and offer some comment, some expression of hope, but the Salem merchant ignored him.

From the rear of the group came laughter, and McCain turned and looked back in time to see a jug being passed around. At this, his displeasure was so great that he spoke to Shute about it.

"They're drinking back there."

Shute turned his head and looked, then said, " 'Pears that way, don't it?"

"This is no time for drink," McCain said.

"Depends on how thirsty a man is," Shute said evenly. "I didn't pick 'em because they'd taken the pledge."

They traveled that day through rolling, wooded country, and occasionally they saw cleared fields and cabins, but Shute always gave them a wide berth. McCain would have stopped and talked, asked questions, but Shute seemed determined not to have this happen. He was in no hurry, yet there was a steady urgency about the man that could not be disputed, and other than brief periods of walking to save the horses, McCain knew that Shute was driving hard, covering a lot of miles.

Toward evening they came to a creek and crossed it, and made their way across a cultivated field to a low cabin beyond. McCain did not recognize the place until the man came out; then he remembered that he had seen him a few times in Salem. With this knowledge, McCain studied the surrounding land more carefully and realized that they were near the Salem-Oregon City trail, and about eight miles north of Salem.

He meant to speak to Shute about this, but Shute had stepped out to meet the settler. They were shaking hands when McCain came up. "Kendall's the name," the man said to McCain. "Your face seems familiar to me. Ain't I seen you before?"

"Perhaps in Salem," McCain said. He spoke to Shute. "We're a bit close to the road, ain't we? By that I mean—"

"We'll camp the night in your yard, Kendall," Shute said. "Have your wife make coffee. Beans will do, and some pork."

Kendall's face faded slightly. "Ain't you fellas got provisions of your own?" He looked at Neal Shute's expression, and added, "I don't mean to sound inhospitable, but—"

"Then don't," Shute said flatly.

"What I'm tryin' to say is, my winter provisions is laid up and intended to feed two." He grinned. "Why, I'd have to make another trip into Salem. Didn't plan on that either."

"Kendall," Shute pointed out, "we're always doing things we never planned on. Now you do as I tell you and come see me at the store." He put his hand on the man's shoulder. "All right?"

"I guess it's got to be," Kendall said, and turned to the cabin, trying to figure out a way to tell his wife she had to cook for twenty-three men. He acted like a man who wasn't sure he could do this.

McCain said, "Shute, we could have fixed for ourselves. There's no need to push hard on a man like that."

"My decision," Shute said. He looked past McCain. Some of the men were pitching Kendall's hay on the ground for beds, and two men had taken his horse out of the lean-to, meaning to use it themselves. McCain's face had his disapproving look.

He said, "These men ought to try that on my place sometime."

Shute seemed amused at the statement. "What would you do, Angus? They'll have their way. Less trouble for everyone to let it go. Some men are like that."

"Yourself included?" McCain asked.

"Myself included," Shute said. "A man doesn't get where I am unless he does for himself. I've hurt men who stood against me. I may hurt more before my life's done." He smiled. "McCain, I've always thought you to be too gentle a man. It's a tough country. Be tougher."

"It's been my view that a man should soften a place rather than toughen to it," McCain said. "Will you win a friend by walking on Kendall?"

"I'm not trying to," Shute said. "McCain, what can Kendall do? Tell me to go to hell?" He shook his head. "He knows he could have a bad year and need credit from me, and it's tough to get after you've had words with a man. Kendall couldn't tell me he didn't have enough to feed us either, because he bought his supplies from me; I knew how much he had."

"Is it right to use a man, squeeze him?"

Neal Shute shrugged. "Hell, I don't know, Angus. But it's a lot better to be that way than to have it the other way around. I know. I've had my tough times and I never liked any of them." He paused for a moment. "I know what you think, Angus; I saw the look on your face when I came back with these men. Well, let me tell you something. The kind of men you need are not the shopkeepers, the men you know. Sure, they'd come. They wanted to come, but I said no because I know them. They'd stay at it a day, maybe two, then they'd get to thinking about their business and they'd wonder if the clerk was dipping in the till. Or they'd get lonesome for their wives and kids, and pretty soon they'd quit you, one at a time. You'd understand, and they'd leave you all alone. These men won't leave you, Angus, because there's two dollars a day in it. Sure, they don't give a hell for you or Tammy, but they'll stick. Now, which would you rather have right now? Your friends, or these no-good bastards who'll stay?"

Angus McCain thought about this, then said, "I sure don't

understand you, Neal. You think of things in a way I never would."

"We lead pretty tough lives," Shute said, "but in different ways. Your way is land-tough, climate-tough. Mine is people-tough. The drummer who tries to take my order wants me to think I'm getting the bargain of the year, but all the time he's trying to make an extra dollar for his own pocket. Kendall seems real put out, but he ain't. He's already figured out that this inconvenience is good for ten pounds of bacon and an extra sack of flour next time he comes into the store. And you know somethin' else? He'll be in Salem to collect in ten days."

The talk made sense to McCain and gave him a better understanding of Neal Shute, but it didn't put him at ease. These men were rough men, noisy, and they liked their liquor. By the time it was fully dark and a campfire had been built, a few of them were well on the way to being drunk. This worried McCain, but then he supposed they got drunk often and would be cold sober in the morning.

Kendall's wife appeared with a large kettle of coffee. She was an attractive woman, a little plump, and McCain felt sorry for her, sorry because she had to endure the remarks of men who had little sensitivity and less respect for a woman.

When she went back to the cabin she was crying, and a moment later Kendall came out in a huff; he carried his rifle and walked rapidly toward the camp set up in his yard. McCain saw him coming and got up, but Shute got there first; he grabbed Kendall and whirled him around and held him until McCain could take away the rifle.

"You fool, Kendall!" Shute said. "You'll just get yourself killed!"

"By God, this is my land and I'll—"

"Shut up and listen to me!" Shute snapped, and Kendall looked wide-eyed. "Nobody hurt your wife. It was just talk. Don't push these men past the talkin' stage. Now you go back to the house. Bring out the rest of the food. Tell your wife to stay inside. You understand that?"

Kendall nodded. "You understand something too. If anyone comes near my cabin tonight, I'll shoot to kill."

"You do that," Shute said. "Give him his rifle, Angus."

McCain handed it to Kendall, who went back to the cabin. He came back a few minutes later carrying a pan of fried pork. He put it down and returned to the cabin and slammed the door. The lamp went out and McCain spoke to Shute. "He won't sleep tonight."

"He'd better not," Shute said, and ate his meal.

The fire was allowed to die out as soon as they were through eating, and the men settled down for the night. McCain spread his blankets on the ground and rolled into them, keeping his rifle with him. Neal Shute slept ten feet away.

For a time McCain remained awake, thinking about Tammy, who was gone, and yet trying not to think about her, for his mind conjured up unpleasant things. Coming across the country in wagons, they'd had some Indian trouble, although McCain had never really figured out why. They had meant no harm to the Indians. They had only meant to cross the land, but the Indians had attacked anyway. Some of the travelers had been killed. Some, the small children, had been taken by the Indians. This was what McCain would never forget, the hysteria that followed.

He remembered the Daniels family. The entire train had been camped on the banks of the Platte, and the wagonmaster, a stern frontiersman, had warned them against letting the children out of the compound formed by the wagons. But some could never take a warning seriously, and the two small Daniels boys had wandered off. There was panic, and Daniels was worse than the others; he broke away, took his horse and rifle, and started out. The wagonmaster, against his best judgment, organized a search party and went after him, and McCain had gone along. Two days later they found Daniels staked out on the prairie, dead. They never found the boys. Later, McCain talked to the wagonmaster, who theorized that the boys were probably taken south and sold to the Comanches.

Now it was Tammy, and a man just wouldn't think it could happen in the valley. But it had happened, and now McCain was on another search party. He blocked his mind against any further speculation, and finally slept.

The sound of a gun going off woke him. He struggled free of his blankets and stood up, looking around in the darkness, trying to figure out where it had come from. Neal Shute, also on his feet, said, "The cabin," and ran toward it. McCain followed him, as did most of the men in the camp.

By the time they got there, Kendall had lighted the lamp; he opened the door and stepped out, his rifle in hand, and his wife shot the bolt. Kendall pointed his rifle at the men gathered there and edged along the wall of the cabin until he came to the window. Then he held the lantern up and they saw the dead man there, blood still oozing from the hole in his chest.

Abe stepped through the front row, looked at the man, then at the window. A hunting knife was still stuck in the putty that held the glass in place, and they could all see where the pane had been worked on. Abe said, "Charlie, he must have wanted some of that woman pretty bad."

Kendall had fired through the window, shattering one pane of glass, and now he looked at these men, wondering how he was going to handle them all.

Neal Shute said, "When a man wants something, then he's got to be ready to pay the going rate." He looked at the men. "We'd better bury him. No need leavin' it for Kendall to do." He turned and held out his arms and they turned too, like chickens being shooed into a coop.

McCain remained with Kendall, who nervously wiped a hand across his face. "Is that all they're goin' to say?" Kendall said.

"What do you want them to say?" McCain asked.

"I—I just killed a man," Kendall said. "One of their friends."

McCain shook his head. "They're not friends, Kendall. Go back to bed."

Chapter 8

Tammy's shoes gave out before she did, and Pete Dannifer stopped, took off what was left of his leather shirt, and made her a pair of Indian wrap-arounds. They had been walking for hours; the day was hot and they didn't seem to be making much headway, but Dannifer knew that each step took them nearer the road, and increased their chances of finding help. It was important to Dannifer to know where he was, not only to get Tammy home as quickly as possible, but to warn everyone about the gypsies; they'd steal hogs and chickens and anything else they could lay their hands on, and vanish unless people were warned in time.

In the middle of the afternoon they came across a she bear

and a pair of year-old cubs in a clearing. Dannifer stopped still, Tammy slightly behind him, and for several minutes they stood there, staring at the bear while the bear stared at them. The wind was in their faces and the bear's poor eyesight couldn't quite make them out. Then one of the cubs came toward them, and Dannifer reached for the knife; he couldn't take a chance of the rifle firing since it had been soaked in the river.

Then the cub caught a whiff of their scent and stopped. A moment later it trotted back and Dannifer suddenly whooped. With a snort the she bear lumbered away, her cubs racing on ahead of her. After they disappeared through the brush, Dannifer let out his breath. "I sure didn't care to tangle with mama bear." He looked at the gun and said, "A man never knows, does he? This thing got dunked, but if he was using a good greased patch and a tight cap, the powder might still be dry." He cocked the rifle, pointed it up into the trees, and pulled the trigger. It bucked and roared and left a cloud of black powder smoke hanging in the clearing, and Pete Dannifer said, "Well, I'll be damned!"

He looked at the rifle, then up through the bordering fringe of trees at the sun to establish the direction. "Care to walk a spell with me?" he asked

"I don't mind if I do," Tammy said. Her hair was tangled and the left side of her face was swollen from the blow on the temple, and dirt remained in the creases by her nose. She laughed as he studied her. "I'll bet I look just stunning."

"Well, you do look unusual," Dannifer said. He scraped a hand over his whiskers, for he had a dense, dark beard. "You know, if we were to tell anyone we was taken with one another, they'd think we were crazy." The humor left his eyes. "When we get you home, things will be different. You might want to change your mind, Tammy. If you do, why, I'll—"

"There's nothing to change my mind about," she said. "If I didn't have sense enough to know what I wanted when I saw it, then I wouldn't be worth having." She took his arm. "Let's walk."

They kept the setting sun behind them; the shadows grew long and the light started to go, and Dannifer began to look for a night campsite. He didn't want to stop for another night, but there was no sense going on in the dark, and it would be that in a little while. Then Dannifer heard a sound somewhere off to the left and he stopped. A moment later he caught sight of a mounted man, and the sighting must have been simultaneous, for the man altered direction and rode over quickly but with caution, for he kept his short-barreled rifle pointed at them.

He was a whiskered man not much older than Dannifer, but his beard was a product of long days on the trail, not a chosen cultivation. He looked at them, then said, "Why, it's a girl!" He swung down and held his horse. "I'm Jake Early of Early and Cogswell, on portage from Portland." He nodded toward the east. "We were movin' along the road when we heard the shot. No one lives in these parts, so I thought I'd better take a look-see. You folks lost? 'Pears like you've had a rough time of it." He turned to the saddle and put up his gun. "We were about to camp for the night anyway. Not far. There's hot grub and I can fix you up with clothes." He smiled. "You can tell me about it then if you want."

"Do you think a bath could be arranged?" Tammy asked.

Jake Early laughed. "Lady, I've got three dozen tin wash-tubs on my pack mules. You're sure welcome to use one."

"How big is your train?" Dannifer asked.

"Sixty mules," Early said matter-of-factly, and turned to lead the way to the road.

Dannifer's first look at the pack train made him think of a regiment of cavalry camping. In addition to the sixty mules, Early had thirty mounted and well-armed men, twelve Indian swampers, five wagons, including the cook wagon and complete trail outfit. Early saw the expression on Dannifer's face and laughed.

"It's big, all right. And getting bigger." He took them to his wagon where a tent had been pitched. He gestured to one of the cook's helpers and said, "Get one of the tubs off the mules. Fetch water, and have two cots set up in the tent; I'll move my stuff outside and sleep under the wagon."

Dannifer opened his mouth, but he wasn't sure what he meant to say first: that he and Tammy weren't married, or that Early didn't have to go to that trouble. He said neither one, for Tammy put her hand lightly on his arm; he looked at her and she said, "It would be best if we slept under the wagon, Mr. Early, but I appreciate the use of the tent for the bath."

"I've already made up my mind," Early said pleasantly. "You don't want to argue with the host, do you?" He took Dannifer by the arm. "I've got a little something to drink over here, and we can talk while your wife's enjoyin' her bath." He led Dannifer over to the cook wagon and uncorked a bottle. It was good whiskey, the kind that burned pleasantly all the way down, and built a banked fire once it got there.

Early called a man over. "Henry, look on the manifests and find those calico dresses Shute ordered. Pick out something blue, for a slender woman, and bring it to my tent."

Henry nodded and walked away. "Sit down," Early offered, motioning to a keg. "I think my clothes will fit you, Mr.— Well, I'll be damned, we didn't get around to that, did we?"

"Pete Dannifer." He sat down and glanced again at the bottle, and Early handed it to him. Dannifer took two swallows and handed it back; he didn't want Early to get the idea that he was a drunk who hadn't had any for a long time. "I'd like to tell you about this." Dannifer said.

"In your own time," Early said.

"Now's a good time. The girl and I met on the Salem road three days ago. Or maybe it was four—I've lost track. Anyway, she was goin' to a settler's place to help bring in a baby. I gave her a ride on my horse and down the road a piece we met some gypsies."

Early frowned. "South of Salem?"

Dannifer nodded and went on. He told of the attack on Wilkerson's place, and of their escape down the river, and he kept it simple, covering the ground quickly, for Early could fill in the details himself without a lot of talk about how tough it had been. When Dannifer finished, Jake Early scraped his beard with his fingers and said, "You don't know how many were in this gypsy band?"

"No, but they were camped on Daniel Shotten's place. You know him?"

"South of Salem? No, I've never been on that road. How the hell did the gypsies get here? The river?"

"That's my opinion," Dannifer said. "I rode alone all the way from San Francisco and I never heard of any gypsy band until a few days ago."

"That's damned odd," Early said. "Usually news of 'em travels like brush fire." He thought a moment. "Did you lose much gear?"

"A pack horse, saddle horse. A pair of Colt's pistols; the usual things a man carries on the trail. It'll take me three hundred dollars to replace everything."

"Sometimes that's more than a man can rake up," Early said. "I've seen that time, Dannifer. I hope you're not caught that way."

"I guess I've got a hundred and fifty in gold on me," Dannifer said. "If there's a bank in Salem I can draw a draft on a San Francisco bank. It'll take a month to come through, but it'll be worth waiting for." He was silent a moment, then added, "In the mother-lode country I staked an old crowbait and damned if we didn't hit it rich. We sold out for thirty thousand dollars apiece."

Jake Early stared. "My God, man, that's a fortune!"

"It sure seems like it," Dannifer said. "There was some betting that I wouldn't get it out of the gold country and into the bank at San Francisco, but we did." He laughed. "The last I saw of the old crowbait, he was tending bar in his own saloon and havin' the time of his life." He looked seriously at Jake Early. "I'd appreciate it if you said nothing to Tammy McCain about this. We ain't had time to get real acquainted, if you know what I mean, and I'll tell her my way, in my own time."

"It's not my business," Early said.

"Neither is the question you're itchin' to ask," Dannifer said. "However, I'll tell you. It was my intention to take a look at Portland, then go back to Texas and live big. But I met her, and somehow things changed mighty rapid. Oregon looks real good to me now and we've come to the agreement that we ought to put up a cabin for the two of us."

"With your kind of money," Early said, "you'll have more than a cabin." He stood up and stretched. The cookfire was bright, and along the road, at even intervals, individual campfires had sprung up. "We'll be in Salem late tomorrow," he said. "I'll send someone on ahead with word that you're with us."

"Make sure the McCain people know," Dannifer said. "Likely they've got a posse out lookin' for her."

"Posse? I never heard that word before. What's it mean?"

Dannifer grinned. "In Texas a posse is a bunch of mounted men set on hangin' the first fella they come across."

Jake Early nodded. "Things ain't much different in Oregon."

Chapter 9

A day and a half of travel took them northeast into an unsettled, densely wooded country of deep valleys and ragged ridges, and to Angus McCain's mind they followed no trail at all. Abe seemed to know where he was going; McCain understood their destination would be an Indian camp, and he wondered how Abe knew of these things. Probably through Shute's trading; he occasionally bought from the Indians, and McCain supposed that he also sold to them.

Finally they cold-camped and Shute called McCain over. "Tanan Two Bear's village is just over the ridge. We'll go the rest of the way afoot."

"How do you know he's the Indian we're after?"

"*I'm* not sure," Shute said. "Abe is. He recognized the headband found at Wilkerson's place."

"Abe seems to know a lot," McCain said.

"Why not? He was a squaw man for seven years."

McCain rather expected they would plan their advance, but no one seemed interested; they left the horses in the care of one man, took their weapons, and advanced up the wooded slope on foot. Abe was leading them, and McCain was content to follow slightly behind. When they neared the top they fanned out, spreading out along the ridge and remaining there while every man had his look. Below was a small valley with a stream bisecting it and the village was on both sides. It was not a large village, but by McCain's guess it contained at least a hundred Indians. There had been a time a few years back when a village held a thousand or more, but the homesteaders had split the tribes up, pushed them out, rooted them around until only small bands remained. He supposed it was smart, for it kept them apart, kept them weak; and when they were weak they weren't inclined to fight.

Shute, twenty yards to the right, had a conference with Abe; then he started to walk down the slope, and there was nothing to do but to follow him. There wasn't much light left, for the sun was down beyond the mountains, and by the time they reached the bottom it was fully dark. A motion from Shute was enough to fan out both ends of the line and the center remained stationary while the ends advanced and in this way, undetected, they encircled the camp.

They moved in together and were at the outer fringe of the lodges before the Indians even knew they had company. Instantly there was a cry and a general stirring, but it was too late, for the men pushed the Indians at gunpoint to the center of camp and held them on both sides of the creek where the big fire threw out light. The women and children were kept back, but two of Shute's men left the main body and walked among them. Abe and Shute stood together, and because it was his daughter they sought, McCain joined them.

Tanan Two Bear came forward. He looked at Shute and McCain, then at Abe, a man he had called his friend. "Why you come?" Tanan Two Bear asked.

"He knows why we've come," a man said.

The two men who had circulated among the women came back with a squaw, and the moment McCain saw her he recognized the dress. Shute was watching him, the question there in his eyes, and McCain nodded. "It's hers all right."

Abe said, "Where's the girl you took, you thief?"

"No girl," Tanan Two Bear said.

"Hey!" one of the men said. "Ain't that Wilkerson's hat?"

"Naw," another said. "That's the doc's. I've seen him wearin' it."

"Bring that Injun forward," Abe said. Two men fought the brave to the fireside and Abe took the hat off his head and looked inside it. "Hell, it's got Mandeley's initials." He looked around, stopping his eyes on Shute and McCain. "Anybody doubt we've got the right Injuns?"

"I want to hear his story," McCain said, pointing to Tanan Two Bear.

"He'll just tell you lies," Abe said.

"I still want to hear it," McCain said. "If he's got the girl, I'm willing to forget the rest, as long as he produces her."

"The girl's dead," Abe said flatly. "And if she wasn't, we make no deals."

"Let the Indian talk," Shute said. He looked at Tanan Two Bear. "Tell the truth."

He did, exactly, and no one believed him. McCain wanted to, but in the end his hurt and rage took over and he couldn't control it; he knocked the Indian down and kicked him and then when the Indian drew his knife, McCain shot him full in the face and rolled the body in the creek.

That shot was a signal. The Indians yelled and started to fight, and Abe's men were ready to fight anyway; they fired point-blank into the Indians, not caring who they hit, as long as they hit someone. The women grabbed up the children and ran screaming from the camp, and the men paid no attention to them. Already a dozen Indians were down, some dead, some dying, and a few trying to crawl away with their wounds. McCain reloaded his rifle; the smell of dying and blood was a fever in him and he shot another one.

Some of the bucks made it free and fired into the wheeling knot of men around the fire, then ran for their lives, and were lucky. But most of them were not lucky; they died there by the creek, or were disarmed and taken prisoner.

As soon as the firing stopped, sanity came back to Angus McCain. He looked around and felt sick. At quick count, twenty Indians were dead, and four of their own men. Several were wounded, but still able to walk.

Six Indians remained, and McCain supposed a few had gotten away—he wasn't sure whether he was glad or sorry. Neal Shute said, "There's a stout tree across the creek. Fetch the rope."

"Wait!" McCain said. "What good will that do now?"

"You want to leave 'em alive?" Abe asked. "Mister, you want to get along with Indians, then you've got to teach 'em a lesson."

"There's been enough killing," McCain said. "More won't bring her back."

"You're wasting your breath," Shute said finally. "Stay out of it if you want, Angus, but don't interfere."

McCain looked at Shute. "And you?"

"It makes no difference to me," Shute said. "Be smart and think of it that way." He put his hand on McCain's arm as though to hold him, and nodded to Abe.

They shouted like joyous children as they dragged the Indians across the creek and flung the ropes over a low branch. They tried to hang all six at once, but the combined weight broke the branch; so they picked another and hung four at a time. McCain couldn't watch; he turned his back and that helped, but he could hear the Indians kicking, their legs fanning the air. He could hear them strangle, for the men used a simple slip knot that did not break the neck and kill quickly.

McCain said, "Who are the real savages here, Shute?"

"There's no difference. I never pretended or thought that

there was." He took a cigar from his pocket and lit it. "It's hard to think of her as gone, McCain. I'm sorry, but I know that's no help to you."

"That's right," McCain said, then he looked hard at Neal Shute. "Did you love her? Really love her?"

"I wanted her for my wife," Shute said.

"That's not the same thing."

"It is to me," Shute said.

McCain sighed. "How will I tell my wife she's gone?"

"Just tell her. What else is there to do?"

Abe and his men came back across the creek. Abe was holding a Colt pistol by the trigger guard. "Found this," he said. "Fancy for an Injun, ain't it?"

"I'll take that," Shute said.

Abe hesitated, then said, "I thought I'd keep it myself."

"You thought wrong." Shute said. He stood there a moment, staring flatly at Abe, and the man handed it over. Shute looked at the pistol as though trying to decide whether to keep it or put a price on it and sell it. Then he thrust it into his belt and reached into his back pocket and took out a pouch; he opened the drawstring and counted out some gold pieces, which he handed to Abe. "I'm not paying for the dead men," Shute said.

"They won't know the difference," Abe said. "See you at prayer meetin'." He looked at McCain but didn't say anything, and McCain understood he didn't care one way or another how any of this had turned out. Abe turned and left the Indian camp, and the men followed him because he had the money.

After they had walked away, McCain said, "Where do you find such men, Shute?"

"Anywhere," Shute said. He started to turn, then thought better of it. "I'll expect you to bear half this cost, McCain. You'd better come along. This isn't the healthiest place to be."

"Do you think I care?" McCain said.

Shute looked at him and smiled and walked on; a moment later McCain followed him. Abe and the others had already ridden out. Shute mounted up and he didn't wait for McCain; he seemed to have lost interest in the man.

Pete Dannifer and Tammy McCain rode into Salem with Jake Early's caravan, and the arrival created quite a stir in the town. Early & Cogswell had a stable and equipment yard, and the train went there. Unloading began immediately; this was taken care of by Early's foremen.

The company had a small log office and to this Early went with Dannifer and Tammy. The elderly man who was in charge came to the door.

"Good trip, Mr. Early?"

"As usual," Early said, and went inside.

The man looked at Dannifer, then at Tammy. "Say, ain't you the McCain girl? Holy smoke, I heard you was done in by Injuns."

Early had been going through some mail, but when he heard this he came to the doorway. "What's this, Ed?"

"Why, Neal Shute and a bunch of roughs rode out of here some days ago. There'd been a massacre at Wilkerson's place."

"The damned fools!" Dannifer said. "It wasn't Indians, it was gypsies."

"Gypsies?" Ed shook his head. "I got it to be Injuns. Shute said so himself."

"The man's a stupid fool if he can't read sign better than that," Dannifer said. "There wasn't an Injun near the place."

Ed shrugged his thin shoulders. "That's your story, but if I could give you a word of advice: I wouldn't tell it around that Shute was stupid, or a fool. He won't like it."

"Do you think I care what he likes?" Dannifer asked. He looked at Early. "Could you loan me a decent pistol? I'm going to take Tammy home and ride on to the Shotten place."

"Better not do that alone," Early advised. "Pete, I've sent a man on. Stay in town the night. I'll ride out to Shotten's with you in the morning. Now that's reasonable, ain't it?"

Dannifer had his own way of doing things, but there was logic in what Early said. Logic, and a strong man's will behind the words. Finally Dannifer nodded and said, "I guess we could put up at the hotel all right with no harm done."

"I keep two rooms there," Early said. "You're welcome to them." He held up his hand. "Now don't argue about it."

Arguing with Jake Early, Dannifer thought, might be some bit of trouble, whether it was friendly or not. "I want to do what's best for Tammy," Dannifer said.

"I reckon this is best," Tammy said. "It ain't gettin' back that matters so much, but just lettin' pa and ma know I'm all right."

Early said, "Ed, go on over to the hotel and tell the clerk I said it was all right if they took my rooms." He glanced at Dannifer. "I'll buy you two dinner tonight."

"All right," Dannifer said.

He took Tammy by the arm and walked her away from the yard to Salem's main street. Most of the buildings were log; only a few of the newer ones were going up as frame and siding, and he wondered about this. He decided that no one had bothered to set up a saw mill; trees were handy, and a log structure went up fast.

The street was still muddy in spots, and they avoided these and crossed over. The hotel was a two-story building halfway down the block and just their passing along caused some talk, for everyone in town seemed to know that there'd been Indian trouble.

Ed was coming out of the hotel; he stopped to talk to a man and then went on. When Dannifer and Tammy approached the door, the man there stopped them.

"Glad to see you got clear of the Indians," he said.

"I was never taken by Indians," Tammy said firmly.

The man smiled and scratched his beard. "Neal Shute said—"

"He was wrong," Dannifer said, interrupting.

The man looked at him and shrugged. "Neal ain't often wrong."

"He is this time," Dannifer said, and they went inside.

The clerk gave them a key and they went up the stairs. Dannifer opened the door for her and said, "You might try to catch up on some sleep."

"What are you going to do?"

"Look at the town," he said. Then he grinned. "If we wasn't standin' in the hall of a public roomin' house, I guess I'd kiss you."

"I didn't think a thing like that would stop you."

"Well, I wouldn't put you to no embarrassment," Dannifer said.

"Is that what's holding you back?"

"Nothin's holding me," he said, and put his arms around her. He kissed her and then released her, and she laughed and patted his cheek.

"Somehow, you never disappoint me," she said, and went inside.

He went down the stairs to the main room and found a fair crowd standing there; they all looked at him as though he were a curiosity. One man said, "The talk's goin' up and down the street that you saved the McCain girl from the Injuns."

Dannifer looked at them and judged them to be the town's businessmen, the substantial citizens of Salem; they did not have the rough, homesteader way of dressing, and for the most part their hair was cut and their beards were trimmed, a sure sign they lived in town and enjoyed the services of a barber.

"No Injuns," Dannifer said. "Gypsies. Ask old man Shotten about it. They were roostin' on his place."

The man who had spoken looked at his friends, then said, "We heard of no gypsies, friend."

"You just did, because I told you," Dannifer said, and pushed through.

He made the boardwalk and stopped, for someone had come out right behind him. He turned and saw a tall man standing there. He was in his forties, a bit grave of expression; a full, drooping mustache hid his mouth.

"Buy you a drink?" he asked.

"Why?"

The man shrugged. "It's a good excuse to talk. I'm Dan Holder. Twice a week I publish a paper in Salem, and dream of the day when I can make it three times a week. Now how about the drink?"

"You want a story?"

"The truth," Holder said.

"That I can give you," Dannifer said, and he crossed the street with Dan Holder and they went into a saloon. The noise, the crowd, told Dannifer that Salem was a booming town, and would continue to boom. It was his experience that an hour in a saloon would reveal more about a town than a week of picking up gossip. If a saloon was quiet during the day and busy on the weekends it usually meant that the town was pretty well settled and all the good jobs had been taken. But if a saloon was crowded during the day, it meant that some men worked at night for good pay, and that just about everything was on the upswing.

Holder got a bottle and two glasses and crossed the sawdust to a table, where they sat, out of the run of the place, but where they could see it all.

"Timber men," Holder said, nodding toward the bar where men stood two and three deep. "They'll go to work at four this afternoon and keep at it until two in the morning. The day crews work the woods and send the logs down the water shutes to the pond west of town. They'll spend half the night making room for the next run."

"Don't anyone around here know how to saw boards?" Dannifer asked. "The town's mainly built of logs."

"Ted McGee's got a ripsawing outfit to the edge of town," Holder said. "But he's too small to handle what this calls for."

"Saw pits?" Dannifer said.

Holder nodded. "You know something about the work?"

"Some. What holds McGee back?"

"Money for steam engine and equipment," Holder said. "Was a man to be the first in here with a steam engine, he'd make a fortune. Neal Shute's been trying to buy one back east. Talk has it that he's about to close the deal and ship it around the Horn." Holder sighed. "Well, you can't stop a man with cash in his hand, I guess."

"Ain't it a shame," Dannifer said.

Holder laughed. "You know the man?"

"I never met him."

"But you don't like him," Holder said. "The girl?"

Dannifer hesitated, then said, "You're smart."

"I wish I were," Holder said. "Tell me what happened at Wilkerson's place."

Dannifer did, making it brief, but not leaving anything out. Holder took a few notes, and when Dannifer was through he said, "I can get out a paper in two and a half hours. Would you understand if I seemed in a hurry?"

Dannifer nodded, and when Holder started to get up he took the man by the arm. "You don't like Neal Shute either."

"That's right," Holder said. "He talks too loud and hits too hard, and maybe a little often to suit me."

"Is McGee easy to find?" Dannifer asked.

Holder frowned briefly. "Yes. Just walk west out of town." He paused as though he wanted to say more, or ask a question, but he held it back and left the saloon.

Pete Dannifer finished his drink and went out. He stood on the walk a moment and looked up and down the street; then he turned right, walked a little way, and crossed to an express office and bank.

A clerk who stood behind a wicket looked up as Dannifer approached, and in the man's quick darting glance was the sum total of his appraisal, and it wasn't flattering to Dannifer.

"Who's in charge here?" Dannifer asked politely.

"I'm in charge, sir," the clerk said. "State your business briefly."

Dannifer paused. "Friend, you're in charge of the inkpots, and if you make more than ten dollars a week I'll be missing my guess. Now I asked you a question, and I didn't want a smart answer. You want to hear it again?"

The clerk stared and swallowed, then nodded toward a back office. "Mr. Huber is owner of the bank, sir. I'll tell him—"

"I'll tell him myself," Dannifer said, and swung the gate aside. He went to a closed door, knocked, and opened it when a man spoke.

Paul Huber was a round man, with a pleasant expression made ridiculous by mutton-chop whiskers. "Yes?"

Dannifer introduced himself and sat down. "You're familiar with the Bank of San Francisco?"

"I've had some occasion to deal with them, yes," Huber said.

"Well, I have thirty thousand dollars on deposit there," Dannifer said. "I'd like to have it transferred here, or a letter of credit drawn up so that I can make use of it."

Huber's attention sharpened. "That's a lot of money." He waited for Dannifer to comment, and when he didn't, he said, "It would take twenty days, maybe a few more for a rider to get through. Depends on what the rains have done to the roads."

"When can you dispatch a rider?"

"For that amount, in an hour," Huber said. "There are some papers to be signed—authorizations, you understand. Do you have anything on you to identify you with the account?"

"A cashier's receipt," Dannifer said. He dipped into his pocket and brought out a small tube of bamboo sealed at both ends with a hard dark wax. He borrowed Huber's letter opener and cut off an end, then shook out a rolled bit of paper. "The Chinese in San Francisco showed me that trick," Dannifer explained. He unrolled the paper and handed it to Huber, who studied it carefully.

"I know this signature," he said. "Mr. Dannifer, you may draw on this amount if you wish. Getting the money will only be a formality."

"Suppose we open an account then," Dannifer said. "Confidential, of course."

"Of course," Huber said. "I'll handle it myself." He went out and came back with some papers and a passbook, and spent some time writing. Then he handed the passbook to Dannifer and said, "If you need money, merely present this to the clerk."

"Can he keep his mouth shut?"

"He likes his job," Huber said. Then he leaned back and laced his fingers together. "You're wealthy, Mr. Dannifer. You ought to invest that money."

"My intention exactly," Dannifer said, and he left the bank.

He found McGee's place, and in the saw pit was McGee, a giant of a man sweating and blowing sawdust that fell on him. He had a log in the ways and was ripping it with long cuts of a two-man saw.

"I'd like to talk to you," Dannifer said, squatting by the pit.

McGee finished the cut, and climbed out, beating sawdust from his shoulders and shaking it out of his hair. He looked at Dannifer, looked down a bit, for he was six four and a solid two hundred and forty pounds of work-hardened muscle.

"Talk," McGee said. "The daylight won't hold for me or no one else. Got none to waste either."

"Dan Holder talked to me."

"He talks to everybody," McGee said.

Dannifer handed him the passbook from Huber's bank and McGee looked at the figure, then raised an eyebrow. "So?"

"A third of that would buy a steam engine and set it up and put you in business."

"That's right," McGee said. "Except for two things. I don't have ten thousand dollars and I couldn't get a steam engine around the Horn ahead of Shute."

"Suppose I could get you one a lot sooner than that? Suppose I put up the money for half of the business?"

McGee thought about it. "I don't know you, or what kind of a man you are." He looked at Pete Dannifer and weighed him. "You're asking for a fight. Shute's got his eyes on a big sawmill operation here. You don't look tough enough to me."

"How tough does a man have to be?" Dannifer asked.

McGee thought about that, and said, "You wouldn't last an hour in a saw pit."

"I might last longer than you think," Dannifer told him. "Are you game enough to try me?"

"What do you mean?"

"I'll saw in the pit as long as you want to pull the other end. And if I do, McGee, we talk business."

"If you last until dark," McGee said, "we'll talk." He turned to the man squatting on the log. "Take the rest of the day off, Mose. We've got a bucko here who thinks he'll like the pit."

"He can have it," Mose said, and hopped down.

Ted McGee spat on his hands and jumped up on the log. "All right, mister, we'll find out soon enough if you're guts or mouth. And I don't want to feel you ridin' that saw. That down cut is going to be strong and long, you hear?"

"I hear," Dannifer said, and went into the pit, sinking to his ankles in sweet-smelling sawdust. He had hardly touched the slick handle when it moved under the powerful pull of Ted McGee.

Chapter 10

Work had always been a part of Pete Dannifer's life, and at the age of fourteen he had held down a man's job, asking no favors and getting none. At times he had worked cattle, but he had cut timber too, and he had mined, the hardrock variety where you grubbed it out with a pick and shovel. He'd skinned mules, worked on the docks, and done just about everything else that made for endurance and hardened the hands.

Work had toughened him, but it had never been work like this. In twenty minutes Dannifer's arms and shoulders protested; they began to ache, and before an hour was up he was drenched in sweat and his upper body was a flame of agony. It was the position that did it, working up and down, bending his whole back to it, pulling down with all the strength he had, then easing up, taking the weight of the saw while McGee made the upward cut.

He was dimly aware that Mose had not left the place, and that other men crouched at the edge of the pit and watched this contest, and only a tough core within him kept him from falling in his tracks. His ears rang, and then his nose began to bleed and he had no vision at all, no consciousness except to continue that terrible pulling of the saw.

How long he worked he did not know, and there was no rest. They would make a cut, drop a plank, walk to the end of the pit and start a new cut, and when they finished the log another was rolled onto the guides and the sawing went on.

Then he became aware of talk, a pair of strong hands were lifting him, and then Dannifer realized that he had been lying in the sawdust. Mose splashed a bucket of water in his face, and Dannifer shook his head and looked around. A dozen men were watching him, strong, hard men with blunt faces, yet some of them were smiling. He saw Ted McGee standing there, sweat coursing down his cheeks; his shirt was darkly soaked with it.

McGee said, "How long, Mose?"

"Nigh onto three hours, Ted."

The men murmured over this. McGee said, "How do you feel, mister?"

Dannifer could feel nothing; a numbness had come over him. He shook his head. "If I rest—a bit."

McGee laughed and shook his head. "You're through, bucko. There's not another good pull in you."

There was daylight left, that much Dannifer became aware of, and it saddened him to think that he had lost. McGee nodded and all the men left the pit. He said, "You've never pulled a saw before?"

"Not in a pit," Dannifer said. "What fiend thought of this?"

"It's hell all right," McGee said. "You ought to work it in the summer when the day is muggy and the flies are biting." He put his hand on Dannifer's shoulder. "My cabin is a spit away. Let me put some linament on you. You'll be like a board tomorrow if I don't."

"I feel like a board now," Dannifer said, and let McGee help him to the cabin. The place was small, a bachelor's place, with little furniture and few creature comforts, but McGee was a clean, methodical man; everything was tidy and in its place.

Dannifer stripped to the waist and stretched out on McGee's bunk while the giant rubbed fire and life back into his muscles. They didn't talk for a while and Dannifer was grateful, because he didn't like being licked.

Finally he said, "I wanted to last. Believe that, McGee. I wanted bad to last."

"Where are you from?"

"Texas."

McGee grunted. "They come tough there. The money you have—you come by that honestly?"

"Mining," Dannifer said. "Struck it lucky in California."

McGee said nothing for a moment. "Well, you got your stake on luck. A lot of men do, but they won't admit it. But from now on it'll be hard work. Any man who works with me puts in a dawn-to-dark day, and he never gets so important that he hires a man to do his job."

Dannifer raised his head and turned it to look at McGee. "Do I understand you right?"

"You do," McGee said. "Mister, I work that pit every day. I know what kind of a man it takes to work it. You said your name was Dannifer. Got a first name?"

"Pete."

"A good name. Short. Hate a long name. It always seemed to me that a man's name ought to be short if he means business. Never knew a man named Alexander that I really trusted." He put the cork in the linament bottle. "How do you feel now?"

"Afire, and god-awful smelly."

"You'll be all right. But keep moving and there won't be any stiffness." He got up and put the bottle away, and Dannifer sat up and put on his shirt. McGee took out a bottle of whiskey and offered Dannifer a drink, then took one and put the bottle back. "You told me I could get a steam engine in thirty days. Where?"

"San Francisco."

McGee shook his head. "I wrote to a firm there. They said nothing was available."

"There's one," Dannifer said. "Sometime back a group of men started to build a steam ferry to go up the Sacramento River to the goldfields, but one of the men skipped with the money. The boat was never finished. She's rough planked and her machinery is there, still in crates. A twenty-five-horse-power steam engine. I think you could buy her for three thousand dollars."

Ted McGee whistled. "Twenty-five horsepower! Why, man, that's enough power—" He stopped and thought about all the work such an engine would do. "But getting it here—"

"I thought of that too," Dannifer said. "Jake Early came in today with his train from Portland. I'm going to eat with him and I think he'd make the portage for you. Well?"

"It'll have to be done damned quietly," McGee said. "If Shute got wind of it—"

"We ought to be able to do it quietly enough," Dannifer said. "I don't think Jake Early has a big mouth."

"A good man there," McGee said. "I'd like to talk to him."

"Then let's go to the hotel," Dannifer said.

McGee put his tools away and Dannifer waited; then they walked back toward the center of town. The day was about done and the first grayness of evening deepened steadily. At the hotel they sat on the porch, and a short time later Jake Early came down the street.

He smiled when he saw McGee and shook hands, then they went inside. "The dining room is small," Early said. "I'll get a table if you'll fetch Tammy McCain."

McGee's eyes widened. "Is she here? I thought the Indians—"

"Didn't Pete tell you?"

"No," McGee said.

Early laughed. "You do know how to keep your mouth shut, don't you?" He filled McGee in quickly, and the big man looked steadily at Dannifer.

"You could have told me this and saved yourself some work."

"I go on my own recommendation, Ted."

"Well, it's the best way."

Dannifer went up the stairs and knocked on Tammy McCain's door; she answered it immediately, and they went down to the dining room. She seemed surprised to see Ted McGee and smiled at him, and Dannifer was pleased to find they were friends; it put a stamp of approval on McGee, marked him in his mind as a special man.

Early said, "Don't they ever serve anything in here but beef stew, potatoes, and greens?"

A waiter heard him and came over. "Got a fine pumpkin pie today. Ten cents a cut."

"Bring the whole thing," Early said, and the waiter left. He looked at McGee, then at Dannifer. "Excuse me for asking, but how did you two get acquainted?"

"He pulled a saw for me," McGee said.

"Top or bottom?"

"Bottom."

Early made a wry face. "No offense, Pete, but how long did you last?"

"Nearly three hours," McGee said.

"You're tougher than I thought," Early said. "Did McGee carry you here?"

"Made it on a bottle of linament and a slug of rye whiskey," Dannifer said.

Tammy smiled. "I wondered what that smell was."

"Working man's perfume," Dannifer said. He looked around to make sure they were not going to be overheard. A few of the other tables were occupied, but no one paid any attention to them. "Jake, how would you like to take twenty-five mules to San Francisco?"

Early said, "I'd do it. What's the cargo?"

"A steam engine," McGee said softly. "Pete knows where he can buy one."

"You're going to buy it," Dannifer said to McGee. "The trip will do you good, and besides, there may be some other pieces of equipment that will have to be bought. You're the one to do that, Ted. Besides, I have some business here that needs to be taken care of."

"I'll go. When could we leave, Jake?"

Early thought a moment. "I was going to pull out tomorrow morning for Portland, carrying produce and grain. I could hold twenty-five mules out and—"

"That's no good," Dannifer said quickly. "Load light, but make an early camp and transfer the load and then head south. Jake, we want to keep this quiet."

"Shute, huh?" He looked at McGee. "Why don't you just break the man in two and throw away the pieces. He likes his bully fights."

"He's avoided that with me," McGee said. "And it would be a bad thing. I could kill him with my hands and there'd be no good come of that. Afterward, they'd sympathize with him and say he had no chance." He shook his head. "The man is best hurt in the place he loves most dear, his pocketbook. Let him buy his engine. I want to see his face when I set up my own."

Jake Early looked from one to the other. "You're partners?"

"Aye," McGee said. "Sudden, you might say, but sound. It's a feeling a man gets in here." He tapped his barrel chest.

Jake Early nodded. The waiter came with their food and they waited until he went away, then Early said, "The three of us seem to have thrown in together. I can't say that it displeases me. I do business with Shute, but I don't trust the man. I don't trust any man who wants it all."

Tammy had listened to this and kept out of it, but now she said, "Who's paying for the engine?"

"I am," Dannifer said.

"That will take a lot of money," Tammy said. She was letting him tell her or not; the choice was his.

"I have a lot of money," Dannifer said. He spoke for all of them to hear, but the words were for her. "It's a hard thing to explain, the way I've felt about this money. Most of my dollars have come hard to me, and never more than I needed to get by. The harder I worked, the less I seemed to make. Ted can probably tell you how that is. Anyway, I staked a prospector to fifty dollars which I'd won in a card game and we went into the hills together, looking for gold. A lot of times I've asked myself why I let him have the money in the first place; good sense told me not to. Then I figured out that I hadn't earned it and I felt uneasy about having it. Well, the luck that brought me the fifty dollars held, because within sixty days we'd filed on a pretty rich claim. We sold it out to a company for thirty thousand dollars apiece. I put the money in the bank in San Francisco and just left it there. And I never felt right about it until now."

He looked at Ted McGee and smiled. "He said something to me an hour ago. He said I'd gotten my stake on luck, but from here on in it would be made on hard work. I knew then that I was doing the right thing, putting the money to work, making it wear off the 'easy-come' feeling I've had about it." He reached out and touched Tammy's hand. "Do you understand, Tammy?"

"Yes, I understand very well."

A boy came in carrying some papers and Jake Early motioned him over. He bought three for a nickel apiece and said, "Dan Holder's hope for Salem." It was a single sheet, printed on both sides, and on the front page was the story of Tammy McCain's escape from Wilkerson's place, and her late arrival in Salem after being picked up by Jake Early's mule train.

McGee read the account, then put the paper aside and ate his stew. "I want to see Neal Shute's face when he reads that. He stormed into town some days back to raise his Indian fighters, and the way I understood it, we were all about to be wiped out in a new uprising." He shook his head. "How could he be fooled that bad?"

"He couldn't," Early said. "Shute is a mule, but he's not stupid." He tapped the paper to draw Dannifer's attention to it. "Did you notice that there's not one word of advertising in there from Shute's store?"

"I knew that Holder didn't like him," Dannifer said.

"He gets his printing done in Portland," Early said. "I bring him a bundle of new handbills every time I come here."

"That's an odd way to do business," Dannifer said.

"It's Shute's way," McGee said. "He has the only store in Salem. You buy at his prices or you do without." He looked at Early. "Jake, I've always wondered why you didn't start up here. You could bring prices down."

"I'm in the freighting business," Early said. "A man gets too many irons in the fire and he burns them." He tapped the paper again. "I don't know whether Dan Holder's a brave man or a fool for printing this. But I do know it's not the story Neal Shute got everybody to believe, and when he comes back and reads it there's going to be some hell to pay." He looked at Pete Dannifer. "He'll come to see you. Know what you're going to say?"

"Depends on what he says," Dannifer said.

McGee sighed. "Neal's a rough-houser. He likes to feel a man's head crack. He likes to see blood on a man's face." He grew thoughtful for a moment. "I made a mistake wearing you out on the saw."

"You didn't make any mistake," Pete Dannifer said. "One way or another, Shute's got to come to me." He looked at Tammy, and then at McGee and Early. "We're going to get married."

McGee sat in silence for a time, then he smiled. "I'm mighty pleased to hear that. You worried me, Tammy, seein' Neal so much. I thought that maybe he was making some headway."

"He thought he was," Tammy said. She reached out and touched Pete Dannifer's hand. "Don't hold anything back if Shute comes to you. He'll come as an enemy. Anything, anyone who stands opposite to him is an enemy. It's the way he is."

"I wonder why Shute said there was Indians?" Early asked absently.

"There was Indians if he said so," Ted McGee said evenly. "Shute's no liar." He looked at Pete Dannifer. "I don't reckon you are either, so I figure the Indians just stumbled onto the place after it was all over."

"That's the way it could of happened," Jake Early said. "We saw considerable Indian activity along the road. It's going to be an early winter and they're restless." He got up and laid a coin on the table. "I leave at dawn, Ted. Meet me at the company yard." He nodded and went out, and Dannifer poured some more coffee for them.

"We want to see Huber tonight," Dannifer said. "What do you think—you want to travel with gold?"

McGee shook his head. "A draft I can draw on the bank would be better. How much am I going to have to spend?"

"As much as you need."

After thinking about this, McGee said, "That's a lot of trust to put in a man." Then he shrugged and picked up his coffee cup. "It's a new country and I guess we don't have time to examine a man's pedigree. You look, judge, and decide, and try to be right. And danged if you ain't most of the time."

Chapter 11

It was dark when Angus McCain returned to his place. He was weary and sick at heart, and he quietly put his horse in the barn and went to the cabin. His wife was in the kitchen when he opened the door; he heard her humming softly, and the oddness of it stopped him.

"Woman," he said, and she jumped and he realized that she hadn't heard him come up at all. He put his hat down, and his gun, and stepped toward her. "How do you find it in you to sing?"

She laughed and ran to him and threw her arms around him. "She's safe! She's in town now. Quincy has gone in to be with her."

He felt weak suddenly and fumbled for a chair and sat down. He got the story from her, in rushes of words, disjointed so that he had to ask her to repeat them and go back, and finally he put it together.

Tammy was alive and well, and this overwhelmed him, but behind this relief was something equally overwhelming, and it clouded his face, erased his pleasure.

When his wife saw this, she sat down across from him. "What is it, Angus?"

"God help us for what we've done," he said, and carefully, not sparing himself, he told her of the raid on Tanan Two Bear's village. Then he sat there, shaking his head. "I must answer for this. We all must answer. I'll go see Shute."

"He led you," she said quickly. "Angus, stay out of it. Let it fall on him."

"I killed Two Bear with my own hand," McCain said. "Do you hear me? I fired the first shot." He looked at her as though he hadn't seen her before. "But gypsies? There are no gypsies around here. God, I saw her clothes in the Indian camp. Saw sign around Wilkerson's place. How could it be anything else?"

She got up and put her arm around him and spoke softly. "Come to bed now. Sleep, and in the morning you'll think clearer."

He looked up at her. "Will I? Do you know what I've started? An Indian war! Some got away. It's started now. And we won't stop it. I brought this to the country with my own hand."

"We'll talk about it in the morning," she said, and made him go to bed. She helped him off with his boots and eased him back and drew a blanket over him; then she went into the other room and sat down again. She knew he was right; there would be Indian trouble now. She didn't want to blame him for it, and she couldn't blame the Indians, and she supposed there were things that happened in which no total blame could be laid at all. Things just happened and you lived with them, or died because of them.

Neal Shute dismounted from his lathered horse and turned him over to the stable boy with curt instructions on how he was to be cared for; that was Shute's way, to use something hard, but to take care of it. His store was a block down from the stable, and he hurried along the walk, pushing some men aside who were slow in getting out of his way.

He had a big place, three large rooms connected by archways, and four clerks worked for him; they were getting ready to close up when he came in. The back room lamps were already turned down and one clerk was pulling the shades over the two front windows. Cal Hardison, who was in charge when Shute was away, came over to the counter.

"Everything's in order, Mr. Shute."

"If it wasn't, you'd be out of a job," Shute said, and bent under the counter to stow his saddlebags. He took a fresh cigar from a counter showcase, and lit it from a nearby lamp. They he took the .44 Colt's pistol from his belt, wiped it off with a cloth, and put it in another showcase holding pistols and knives. "Put a fifty-dollar price tag on this, Cal. You don't see many of them, and if a man wants a heavy-calibre pistol he'll be willing to go fifty dollars."

Hardison nodded his bald head and didn't ask where the pistol had come from; he rarely asked anything, just listened when Shute spoke.

"If you're locked up, you can go," Shute said.

"Yes, sir. Early's train came in this mornin'. The Portland mail's on your desk. And Holder's paper."

Shute looked up. "What day is this?"

"Friday."

He frowned. "'Doesn't his paper come out Tuesday and Thursday?"

"Maybe he's going to three days a week," Hardison said, and let himself out. Shute went over and locked the door behind him, then went into the back room, which was his office and living quarters.

He went through the mail, looking particularly for eastern mail, and found a few letters he wanted. One from a machinery company drew his first attention and he ripped it open and read it.

Neal Shute, Esq.
Salem, Oregon Territory

Dear Sir:

Yours of the twenty-first instant at hand. Please be advised that your draft for two thousand, eight hundred dollars has been credited to your account. The Atlas engine, upright, wood burning, of eighteen horsepower, is crated and waiting shipment pending advice from you.

> Y'r M'st Ob'd'nt Servant
> Fulmer A. Paulson
> Atlas Company, Ithaca, N. Y.

Shute laughed and rolled the cigar to the corner of his mouth, and sat down and wrote a letter. He sealed it and put it in his coat pocket and made a mental note to give it to Jake Early tonight; the man was in the habit of leaving at dawn, and Shute planned to sleep a little later than usual.

He looked at his other mail, checked the day's receipts, and then picked up Dan Holder's paper. His eye immediately caught the article and he read it; he read it again before ball-ing the paper and flinging it across the room. He gnawed on his cigar and let his temper have a short run, then he got up and left the store and walked down the street to the small printing shop Dan Holder owned.

The place was dark, so Shute moved up and down the street, checking first the hotel lobby and the dining room; when he failed to find Holder there, he went over to the saloon. There was a lively crowd and it took a moment or two to sort Holder out; the man was standing at the bar, talking to Ted McGee and another man Shute had never seen before.

Without hesitation, Shute moved through the crowd and stepped between these men, stepped between their talk; he looked at Holder, towered over him, and his expression was dark.

"You print lies in your damned paper," Shute said.

"We were just discussing that," Holder said pleasantly. He leaned against the bar and thrust both hands in his coat pockets. "It's our conclusion that the Indians came around later, by accident, and were blamed for something they didn't do."

"I don't give a damn for your conclusions," Shute said. "I know what I saw."

"Tammy McCain says it was gypsies," Holder said evenly. He was wary of Shute, but seemed to have no real fear. Around them men grew quiet, and the quietness spread until a thick silence hung in the room; even the men in the far corner could hear every word that was said.

"She's never seen a gypsy," Shute said. "How would she know, a young girl, inexperienced in the world, and frightened too?" He laughed. "I don't have to take a scared woman's word."

Holder shrugged, and Pete Dannifer said, "I was with her. Do I look scared?"

Shute turned his head and stared at Dannifer. "Who the hell are you, anyway?" He stood there, heavy shoulders bunched, waiting, and when he got no answer, he snapped, "I asked you something!"

"Ask me nice," Dannifer said.

There was a tightening of Shute's expression. "You want trouble with me?"

"What have you got to offer?"

A few men, who had seen Shute fight, drew in their breath sharply, and even Ted McGee glanced at Dannifer as though checking to see whether he was in his right mind.

"I'm too busy to bother with you now," Shute said, and

swung back to Holder. "You print lies. That's twice I've said it. Now you put a new paper out saying that you made a mistake."

"Tuesday's press day," Holder said, "and I have enough local news to fill it." He looked steadily at Neal Shute. "No statement."

"I'm going to have to teach you," Shute said and fisted a portion of Holder's lapel, then he stopped suddenly, frozen where he stood. Slowly, carefully, he looked down and saw the double-barreled pistol pushed against his breastbone.

Dan Holder said, "I carry this all the time. It's not heavy and I've only shot it once before, and only when a man crowded me badly. You may notice that the barrels are barely three inches long, but they're damned near a half-inch to the bore and packed with solid lead ball and ample powder. This little piece makes one hell of a bang when it goes off, but in this case, standing against it as you are, I imagine it will be some quieter. Do you want to hear it?"

Shute took his hand off Holder's coat and stepped back. "A man defends himself with his fists!"

"A man defends himself the best he can," Dan Holder said. "When I hunt bear, I take along a big-bore Sharps. Now I'm not going to be bothered by you, Mr. Shute. Not tonight or tomorrow or any other time. Is that clear?"

For a full minute, Neal Shute stood there, looking at Holder, and the smaller man looked back without a change of expression. Then Shute wheeled, meaning to face Pete Dannifer again, but he rammed full tilt into Ted McGee, who had changed positions along the bar.

McGee stared at him, and there was no more give in him than in a huge sugarpine bole. "You're tryin' to stand where I'm standing." McGee spoke pleasantly enough, but the warning was clear to Shute. With his elbow, McGee pushed Neal Shute back a step, then motioned to the bartender for service. "Give Mr. Shute a drink."

"I buy my own!"

"Suit yourself," McGee said. Then he looked around at the crowd. "Quietest bunch I ever saw. You fellas forget how to have fun?"

"We're havin' fun," one man in the back said. "Shute ain't, though."

Because he was a proud man, Shute stood on his toes and tried to single that man out so he could deal with him later; he was the kind of a man who wanted to fight them all.

Pete Dannifer eased past McGee and said, "Before you go, I want to tell you something. All along now you've had the idea that you were goin' to marry Tammy McCain. Better forget that, because I am."

"That's a lie," Shute said.

Dannifer frowned. "Now there you go again. Is that all you can say? Mister, I'm savin' you the trouble and embarrassment of havin' her tell you." Shute started to raise his hand and Dannifer's voice took on an edge. "Now I don't have a gun on me, but if you put your hand on me I'm going to surprise the hell out of you."

There was no match here for weight, or even size; Shute had forty pounds on Pete Dannifer, and a good two and a half inches in height; yet Shute hesitated and the men in the saloon saw it and would remember it, for Shute had never hesitated before. Some thought that it was Holder behind him and Ted McGee's bulk idly leaning against the bar, but others knew it was not.

McGee said, "I know you, Shute. If you went after Indians, then you got Indians. Tell us about it."

It all came too fast for Shute; he'd started out to have it his way and nothing had come to him. He looked at McGee and said, "Read about it in Holder's damned paper."

"How many Indians did you kill?" Holder asked. "Where's your outfit? Did they come back with you, or did they light out before someone hung them?"

"Ask McCain," Shute snapped. "He was there. He fired the first shot and killed Two Bear." Then he whipped out with his hands and went through the crowd and out of the saloon.

It was a moment before the talk started again, and then it was as though a machine had been halted and put into motion again; Holder, McGee, and Dannifer turned to each other and the others split into groups and the whiskey went over the bar and everything returned to normal.

"There must have been a fight," Holder said. "McCain? He never struck me as the kind who'd lose his head."

"He probably thought he'd lost the girl," McGee said. "Well, maybe we'll have some Indian trouble this winter."

Neal Shute hurried down the street to Jake Early's company compound. The place was lighted by lanterns on poles planted about the yard; Shute saw Early by the door of the office, checking some freight manifests and he went over.

"Here's a letter I want mailed in Portland. See what you can do about getting it on a fast coast schooner."

"Glad to," Early said. "I'm leaving in the morning."

"There's time for some sport tonight, if you've got a man who'll go with me," Shute said.

Early frowned and said, "I suppose you'll put up the purse?"

"A hundred dollars in gold," Shute said. "Ten rounds, cut and claw."

"Well, if a man's fool enough to do it," Early said, "I'm not fool enough to try and stop it. I'll pass the word around. Where?"

"In the stable yard in an hour," Shute said. He jabbed Early on the chest with his finger. "Find me a man, you hear? This town needs some excitement."

"All right. How much do you make off these damned brawls? Or don't you do it for money?"

"Careful with your mouth," Shute said. "I might pick *you*."

"Yes, you might," Early said. "And that might be something to see."

Neal Shute laughed. "Damn it, one of these days I may try you."

"You'll have to find a better reason than money.'

"Maybe you'll give me a reason."

"I'll think about it," Early promised, and went back to his freight manifests. He watched Shute leave the yard, then went to pass the word along to his foreman; there would be, he figured, a man stupid enough, or broke enough, to take Shute up. There always was.

Early found a man, a burly mule-skinner who had no fear and had a desire to earn a hundred dollars. He took the man to the stable yard across the way, where a group of men were stretching rope to form a ring and hanging lanterns so there would be enough light for everyone to see.

Already an early crowd was forming, passing between two men who took their money and waved them to any vantage point where they could get a clear look at the fight. Some sat on the pole rails, and a few wheeled two wagons around and stood on them, while others clustered around the ring and watched it go up.

A dollar a head just to see a man beaten half to death, Early thought, or maybe they paid the dollar to see it go the other way around.

Chapter 12

Quincy McCain came to the hotel as soon as he reached town; he had his father's wagon. Pete Dannifer crossed from the saloon just as he pulled up, and he stood to one side while the boy hugged his sister and tried not to cry. Then Tammy took Quincy by the arm and said, "This is Pete Dannifer."

Dannifer shook hands solemnly, and Quincy pawed a sleeve across his nose, a little ashamed of letting his feelings go. "I'm sure pleased to meet you," he said. "Ma sent me to fetch Tammy home."

"Then I guess you'd better do as your ma says."

"I've got a rifle in case there's trouble," Quincy said. "I ain't scared of nobody."

The fact that he said that at all told Dannifer that the boy was worried, so he said, "Why don't you put up for the night and travel in daylight? I'm going that way myself in the morning, and I'd ride along if you didn't mind."

"Gosh, that would be—" He stopped a moment. "All right. I don't mind the company."

"Good," Dannifer said, and looked down the street. Neal Shute was pushing along through the crowd and he came onto the porch with a bound that skipped the steps.

He saw the boy and Dannifer and ignored them, coming right up to Tammy as though he meant to grab her. But he didn't. He said, "It's a relief to me to see that no harm's come to you. How'd you get that bruise on your face?"

"In the rapids," she said. "Have you met—"

"Yes," he said brusquely, not even glancing at Dannifer. "Tammy, I want to talk to you." He waited for her to invite him inside where they would have privacy, but she didn't, and he wasn't going to ask her right out to do it. "This is a lie, what this man says. You know how I've felt about you?"

"No, I only know how you feel about yourself," she said.

"There was no mistaking my intentions."

"I doubt that anyone could mistake your intentions," Tammy said. "Neal, if I've hurt you, I'm sorry, but I don't think I have. I've made a choice, and I won't change my mind."

"You don't know your own mind," he said. "Tammy, *I've* decided too, and there's no changing that."

From the side, Pete Dannifer said, "I'm getting tired of hearing you talk."

Shute's response was sudden; he whirled and swung, fully expecting his fist to land on Dannifer's jaw, but he didn't connect at all. The fist grazed Dannifer's ear, then he grabbed Shute's arm, whirled, blocked him with a hip, and used the man's own momentum to fling him up and over and completely off the porch.

Shute struck the street at the foot of a passing horseman and nearly got trampled, and there was a flurry of excitement then and a crowd gathered instantly. Shute was rolling, coming to his hands and knees, and he stayed that way a moment as he looked at Dannifer.

Then he swore and charged, racing for the porch, and Dannifer stood there as though he just intended to let the man come on. At the last moment, Dannifer jumped up a little, caught the overhead crossbeam and swung his feet straight out. Both soles of his boots caught Shute flush in the face and the man did a complete somersault backward in the air and landed again on his face in the street.

A whoop went up along the street, and some of the men urged Shute to get up, to get to fighting, but all he could do was roll over, and when he did he revealed the damage Dannifer had done. One cheek was cut to the bone, his nose was bleeding, and there was a deep cut over his eyes, running nearly across the forehead.

The horseman who had stopped to see all this said, "That didn't last long now, did it?" Then he eased his horse around and dismounted, and Dannifer saw the star pinned to the vest; it had been hidden by the open fold of the man's coat. He stepped onto the porch and said, "I'm Cotterage, marshal from Portland. You wouldn't get away with that in my town."

"Then I'm lucky I'm not in your town," Dannifer said.

Cotterage was tall and slender and he turned and looked at the crowd and at Neal Shute, who was still unconscious. "Ain't nobody going to help him?"

"Nobody likes him," Dannifer said.

The marshal shrugged; this was none of his business. "Who's the law around here?"

"I don't know as there is any," Dannifer said. He looked at Quincy. "We got a marshal or anything?"

"No," Quincy said.

This annoyed Cotterage; he pushed his hat to the back of his head and sighed. "That's a heck of a note. Who's important in this town?"

"He is," Dannifer said, motioning to Shute. The man was beginning to stir, and they watched him sit up and fall over and sit up again. Finally he got unsteadily to his feet and looked around, but the blood in his eyes hampered his vision.

Shute said, "Just point me in his direction, someone."

"He's a glutton for punishment, ain't he?" Cotterage said. Then he pointed to a man standing on the edge of the crowd. "Take that man to a doctor."

"We ain't got none."

"Not even a horse doctor?"

"Well, the fella that runs the stable is pretty good." Then he grew indignant. "Hell, get someone else."

"I'm telling you," Cotterage said, but for a moment it didn't look as if he was going to get his way; then the man took Shute's arm and steered him down the street. As they started to move off, a man in the crowd yelled and they stopped.

"Shute's supposed to fight some mule-skinner in an hour!"

"He's had his fight," Cotterage said, and motioned the man on. Then he turned back to Dannifer. "Ain't anyone in this town responsible?"

"Responsible for what?" Dannifer asked.

"Well, for law and order. We had a band of toughs around Portland who tried to pass off as gypsies, and the word I got was that they were heading this way. I figured we could get up a posse and round 'em up. I want one called Romaine for a killing, and two others for strong-arm robbery."

"I can talk to you," Dannifer said. "Come on over to the saloon. I want to introduce you to McGee and Dan Holder." He reached out and patted Tammy on the arm. "I'll see you at breakfast."

He would have turned and left her then, but she seized his arm and pulled him back. She smiled and said, "I want Neal Shute to hear about this," and she put her arms around him and kissed him in front of a hundred amused onlookers.

Then she stepped back, and he grinned. "You put the brand on me good, didn't you?"

"Is there any other way?"

"No," he said, and crossed over with the Portland marshal. When they reached the walk on the other side, Dannifer stopped as Jake Early came down the street. Early saw Cotterage and smiled.

"Didn't expect to see you here, Elmer. Come in. I'll buy you a drink." He frowned at Dannifer. "Didn't I see Shute being led down the street?"

"Yep."

"Well, what the hell happened? Horse-tromped?"

"He took a swing at me," Dannifer said, "and I showed him some Comanche fighting tricks."

"I'm sorry I missed that," Jake Early said, and went inside.

McGee and Holder were still there, but they were at a side table, a mug of beer at hand, and a half-filled pitcher on the table. Jake Early introduced the Portland marshal, and they sat down.

Holder said, "What was all the excitement on the street?"

Early glanced at Dannifer and his eyes were bright; he wanted his joke and would have it. "Oh, a fight."

"Happens every night," Holder said, and sipped his beer. "If anyone lost an eye or an ear, it's worth a few lines in the paper. Really, I ought to do an editorial about all the fights that go on here. Maybe we could get some law and order."

Jake Early said, "Oh, I don't think it was that serious, Dan. But he was pretty beat up. I saw a fella leading him off down the street. What struck me as unusual was that it's usually the other fella who's been led away."

There was a slight increase in Holder's attention. Ted McGee said, "All right, who got whipped?"

"Neal Shute," Early said, and lit a cigar in the moment of stunned silence. When he looked at them he found them staring, not believing him. He laughed and said, "It's a fact. I didn't see it—"

"Well, then—" Holder began, dismissing the whole thing.

"I saw it," Elmer Cotterage said quietly, and this threw a new focus on the thing. He glanced at Pete Dannifer. "I was coming down the street and I happened to be glancing at the hotel when I saw this man, Shute, take a swing at this man here. The next thing I knew, Shute was sailing out into the street. Naturally, as a lawman, when I see a fight making, I head in that direction. As it was, I was close enough so that my horse nearly trampled Shute. Anyway, he got up, charged the porch and got knocked into the street again. That time he didn't get up." He looked again at Dannifer and laughed. "That was a good trick, catching a beam and swinging on it that way. I'll try to remember it."

McGee waited for Holder to say something, and Holder waited for Dannifer, and finally Early bridged the gap of silence. "Ain't anybody going to order some more beer?"

Holder laughed and got up and went to the bar. When he came back he set out glasses and another full pitcher. As he sat down he put his hand on Dannifer's shoulder. "Ted told me about how you worked in the pit. But this is the surprise."

"Shute put me down as easy," Dannifer said. "That was his mistake, and he won't make it again." He filled a beer glass and blew the foam off it. "In Texas, my daddy used to use fellas like Shute for fence posts. It don't do for a man to brag too tough. He'll always run into a man who can teach him a trick or two."

"You'll have to fight him again," McGee said. "He'll make you fight him." He leaned forward and folded his big hands. "And he'll make sure it's on his ground, done his way."

"Well, we'll see," Dannifer said. "The marshal here says that those gypsies are a bunch of toughs that gave him trouble around Portland."

Early looked up. "Romaine?" The marshal nodded. "I didn't see a sign of anything on the trail, Elmer."

"You're too big to tackle," Cotterage said. "He likes a lone traveler. He's been around here then?"

"He died here," Dannifer said, and told the marshal how he had killed the man when he tried to take Wilkerson's cow back from old man Shotten. He went on and told the marshal about the raid on Wilkerson's place, and their escape down the river.

Cotterage nodded. "It all makes sense. Romaine had two brothers. They probably hit you at night for revenge. I see no other reason at all for it." He looked around the table. "I want to talk to this man Shotten."

"Then you come with me in the morning," Dannifer said. "I've got some questions I want him to answer. And he's gonna answer 'em."

A man pushed his way through the crowd and came up to their table; he was a little man in a soiled plug hat and a coat a bit shiny at the cuffs.

"Excuse me, gents, but I've got a bit of a problem."

"We've all got problems," Holder said. "What's yours?" He looked at Dannifer. "This is Curly, one of Shute's flunkies."

"It's about the fight," Curly said. "Mr. Shute's feeling none too good and there's a lot of people at the stable who paid to see the fight and—"

"And now there's not going to be any," Holder concluded. "I assume that Shute put up the usual hundred dollars?"

Curly nodded.

"Simple then. Pay the lucky man the hundred dollars and give everyone their money back."

"Why, I couldn't do that," Curly said. "Mr. Shute wouldn't like it."

"It seems to me," Holder said, "that this has been a bad night all around for Mr. Shute. He's started what promises to be an Indian war, lost his girl, and got knocked out. Now a hundred dollars can't hurt him much more."

"I was talkin' with some of the fellas," Curly said, "and we thought that maybe this fella"—he looked at Pete Dannifer —"could fight the mule-skinner."

Dannifer laughed and shook his head. "Curly, I only fight when I'm crowded into it. Nobody crowds me into fighting a working man who's hungry for a hundred dollars."

"I just don't know what to do," Curly admitted.

"Then I'll tell you," Jake Early said flatly. "You pay my man his hundred dollars or I'll call together my crew and we'll take that hundred dollars, penny by penny, out of your damned hide." He stood up and pointed at the man's nose. "Shute came to me with his hate, looking for someone to maim tonight. Well, he got a man, and I took his damned rough mouth to boot. Now it's turned around. Pay up, Curly, or you'll buy yourself more damned trouble than you ever knew existed."

"I guess there's nothin' else to do," Curly said, and went out.

Early sat down again and drank his beer. Cotterage said, "What's this about Indian trouble?"

"We'll have to talk to Angus McCain about it," Holder said. "He was with Shute. It seems they thought Tauan Two Bear raided the Wilkersons, and they paid him back."

"How many were killed?" Cotterage asked, as though he feared the answer.

After a hesitation, Ted McGee said, "Knowing Shute, I'd say all. Maybe some got away."

"You'd better hope that none did," Cotterage said. "The killing's bad enough, but if someone escaped to carry the tale

—" He shook his head and drained his beer glass. "Any beds left at the hotel? If so, I'll sleep some and see you in the morning."

Chapter 13

Bear Who Walks walked forty-six miles with a bullet in his thigh, and he made the last eighteen miles alone, for Fox Waiting, who started the journey with him, died from the wound in his side. Bear Who Walks was a young man, barely nineteen summers, and he was full of anger, which gave him strength to go on, to stagger into the village of Running Horse. His arrival caused a flurry of excitement, and Bear Who Walks was taken immediately to the chief and was given food and water. While all the many braves gathered around, he told his story of the raid, describing in detail the terror and the injustice of it all.

Running Horse was an ancient man, wise to treachery, and his decision was made long before Bear Who Walks was taken away to rest.

There would be dancing for two days, and a big feast; the hunting parties would be called in, and they would make war. It was a decision immensely popular, for the braves wanted something like this so they could distinguish themselves and take a new name; and after the battles there would be much singing and dancing and feasting. The medicine men welcomed war, for it gave them an opportunity to work their charms and potions and they would become rich, for a charm to protect the wearer from harm was worth many pelts.

The Indians put aside thoughts of hunting, thoughts of laying by stores for the long winter, and they drove south in a sweeping series of raids. They wiped out a homesteader, his wife, and two small children, burned his place, and passed on, killing another family before the word spread that an Indian attack was even under way.

That they were miles north of Tanan Two Bear's country mattered little to them. That they killed innocent people who never knew why they died did not enter their minds. This was war.

Shotten left his place at dawn and took the Salem road, riding a gray-back mule. He had not gone ten miles before his sharp ears picked up the sound of horsemen approaching. Quickly he left the road and took to the timber, where he dismounted and hid his mule in the bushes. He could see the road, and he crouched, rifle in hand, while they came into view. He recognized Pete Dannifer and suppressed the urge to take a shot at him because there was another man with Dannifer, a hawk-faced man who rode with his hand on his rifle. The wagon followed, with Tammy riding beside her brother, who drove.

They passed on and Shotten waited a while, then got his mule, mounted, and cut back to the road and went on into town. He stopped at Shute's store and the clerk told him that Shute was in, but wouldn't see anyone. Shotten hadn't ridden so far to hear that, and he pushed past the clerk and went to the back where Shute had his living quarters.

When he opened the door and saw Shute in bed, he was appalled at the damage to the man's face. Both eyes were puffed badly, and his forehead was heavily bandaged, and Shotten figured it would take at least three weeks for Shute's smashed lips to heal properly.

Shute turned his head and looked at Shotten. He said, "You damned bungler! You told me you could handle Romaine."

"Romaine's dead," Shotten said. "That fella killed him, the one who got away from Wilkerson's with the girl." He leaned against the door. "What happened to you? Horse-kicked?"

"I made a mistake judging a man," Shute said. "Did you see Holder's damned paper?"

"No, I just come to town. Can't read, anyway."

"He called you some fine names, I can tell you," Shute said. "If you was any kind of a man, you'd put a whip to him. The man's got to be taught a lesson." He raised himself on an elbow. "I want you to take care of that, Shotten. Hurt him good. Make him afraid to print any more damned lies in his cheap one-page paper."

"I can do that," Shotten said, and smiled. "I get tired of beatin' on Muley. The change'll do me good. And Holder ain't very big either."

"He won't lay a hand on you," Shute said convincingly. "Then you go on home and quit worrying. Romaine's bunch cleared out?"

"I guess they're some place on the river," Shotten said. He

started to open the door, but changed his mind. "When am I going to get paid?"

"After you take care of Dan Holder."

"I'll be back then," Shotten said, and went out. He stopped at the saloon for a drink, and then went down the street to Holder's small newspaper office. Holder was alone, patiently composing a front page, and he looked up casually as Shotten's shadow darkened the door. Then Holder stood up quickly and said, "By golly, I want to talk to you, Shotten."

"You talked too much already," Shotten said, and bounded into the shop.

Holder was caught behind the counter and he shoved hard on the case of type he was setting; the edge caught Shotten at the belt line and drove him back, giving Holder enough time to escape the cramped quarters behind the counter.

Shotten swore and swung. He knocked Holder back and went after him, grabbing him by the throat, and by sheer strength forced him to his knees. Holder's face was red and his eyes were bulging as Shotten struck him in the face. The commotion drew the attention of passers-by and they stopped at the doorway, but made no move to help Holder.

With his ears ringing and his senses leaving him, Holder fumbled for his pocket beneath the leather apron and he came up with his two-shot derringer. He pressed the muzzles under Shotten's breastbone and pulled both triggers.

The gun popped and Shotten reeled back, both hands clutched to his wound. He looked at the blood squeezed out through his fingers; then his eyes rolled and he fell in a loose heap.

Holder leaned against the counter and sawed for wind, and finally enough strength returned so he could stand unsupported. He said to the men looking in, "Who does a man call at a time like this, anyway?"

"Best thing to do," one man said, "is to dig a hole and bury him."

"Someone ought to tell his boy," Holder said.

"Hell, it'll be the first good news Muley ever got," the man said, and turned away. The others lost interest and left Dan Holder standing there.

Angus McCain wept when he embraced his daughter. They all went into the house, and he kept looking at Dannifer and Elmer Cotterage, but said nothing; he acted as though they were intruding, yet he was too polite to ask them to leave.

Tammy's mother wanted to talk, and her father wanted to talk, and they tried to do so at the same time, so she sat down at the table and made them sit too, and she calmed them. They wanted to hear every detail of her escape, and she told them.

When she was through, her mother said, "My, what a terrible experience."

Elmer Cotterage said, "Mr. McCain, I guess you've had a terrible experience too." He showed his badge. "I'm the marshal at Portland. Since there's no law around here, I mean to get at the bottom of the attack on Two Bear's village."

"It wasn't his fault!" Mrs. McCain said defensively.

He glanced at her. "It was somebody's fault; we know that. Shute says that McCain fired the first shot and killed Two Bear. Is that so or not?"

"It's one of Shute's lies!" she snapped.

"Let him answer," Cotterage said quietly. "Well, McCain?"

"Aye, the first shot was mine," McCain said wearily. He looked at Cotterage. "Man, do you have to talk of this now?"

"Yes," Cotterage said. "It's an Indian war you've started. If it leads to killin', you're responsible."

"How can you say that?" Mrs. McCain asked. "He was taken with grief and—"

"Oh, shut your mouth, woman," Angus McCain said. "It doesn't matter what reasons a man has. I could have learned what there was to learn without killin' the Indian. Am I under arrest?"

"Yes," Cotterage said. "However, it wouldn't be wise to leave your wife and daughter here alone. Stay on your place until it's time to stand trial for what you've done."

"I'm going back to town to live," Tammy said.

Her mother glanced at her. "You'll do no such thing," she said, thus dismissing the subject.

"I've already decided," Tammy said. "I'm to be wed."

Her father and mother stared at her, and Angus McCain said, "If Shute thinks—"

"Not to Shute," Pete Dannifer said quietly. "She's weddin' me."

"And who are you?" McCain asked. "By God, you can't come in my house and make a statement like that!"

"I'd welcome your permission," Dannifer said, "although the lack of it wouldn't keep us from marryin'. We met along the road, and kinda took a likin' to one another. I don't guess there's much more to say about it. The marshal and I've got to go down the road to the Shotten place. On the way back I'll stop for her."

"She ain't leavin'." Mrs. McCain said.

"I'll be ready," Tammy said. Her mother stabbed her with her eyes, and Tammy said, "Ma, it's my way this time. You can't fight that."

"You got no right to leave now, with the mess you got your pa in!"

"Do you really believe that?" Tammy asked. Her mother didn't answer, and Tammy stepped over to Dannifer and put her hands on his arms. "Take care at Shotten's."

She raised on her toes to kiss him, and her mother gave an outraged cry and jerked her around. Tammy's eyes grew dark but her voice was very soft. "Ma, don't you ever lay a hand on me again, do you hear?" She stood there while her mother retreated a step, then she kissed Dannifer and he went out.

Cotterage said, "I'll be back. Good day to you." He found Dannifer waiting by the horses. "These family squabbles blow over quick," he said, and swung up. Then he laughed. "Of course, I don't have a family, and I'm the biggest liar in Portland."

As they rode along, Dannifer felt like a man who had traveled a long, circuitous route. He looked long at the place where he had stopped to feed the cats, that place in his life where he had joined his lot with Tammy McCain's. When a man did a spur-of-the-moment thing, he rarely realized how far-reaching the effect might be.

Farther along, Dannifer said, "I met Romaine here. He stopped me, but he didn't like the looks of my pistol. Do you suppose he had robbery in mind?"

"He's a highwayman," Cotterage said. "A lone man travels these roads at his own risk. The problem has been so bad that there's an attempt being made to bring in the army from San Francisco." He shrugged. "But of course, everyone in a new territory wants the army to come in and set up camp. They keep the Indians and the lawless down, and open up a place for more settlers. Then, too, the army eats, and lets out some pretty good contracts for forage, food, and hauling. Fellas like Shute make their fortunes off the government."

He rode a way in silence. "If we have a general Indian uprising, I guess we may need the army after all. One thing you may notice about these settlers: they ain't too anxious to leave their stores and farms to go fight Indians. There's no money in it. It's a hell of a way to get prosperity, but there's always a land boom and money boom when there's Indian trouble. A couple hundred soldiers need barracks and they get paid and they spend it. Maybe McCain started it, but he can stop worryin', because there won't be twelve men in this country who'd return a guilty verdict for shootin' an Indian."

"Which you figure is too damned bad," Dannifer said.

"Exactly," Cotterage said.

The Shotten place seemed deserted, yet there was smoke coming from the chimney. They rode into the yard and dismounted, and approached the open door. They stopped when they heard a man sweeping and cursing. Dannifer looked in and saw Muley busy raising dust with a broom, and talking to himself while he worked.

Dannifer's bulk blocked some of the light from the doorway and Muley jumped in surprise, but he grinned when he recognized Dannifer. "Why, howdy there. I was just cleanin' up the awfulest mess a man ever saw."

Then he saw Cotterage and grew quiet, not sure what he should do. "I guess you come to look at the cats, huh?"

Cotterage started to speak, but Dannifer got there first. "Why, yeah, Muley. How they gettin' along?"

"Just fine. They see pretty good now. I keep 'em in the lean-to because pa won't allow no dirty animal in the cabin." He stepped outside and walked to the lean-to, talking all the while. "It don't seem right to me, 'cause them little cats they dig a hole and make their mess in it and cover it up so's you wouldn't know it was there, and pa he's like a damned hog—he messes and lays in it."

"You're cussin', Muley," Dannifer said. "Ain't your pa at home?"

"Naw, he left for town this mornin', right after all them fellas left."

Cotterage opened his mouth again to speak, but Dannifer shook his head slightly. Muley missed this and explained: "The other night a whole swod of men come here. They ate everythin' in sight and drunk up all the likker pa had and talked and yelled and a body couldn't get his rest. They was tellin' pa about raidin' some Injun camp, but I never believed that. We got no Injun trouble." He squatted and called his kittens, and they came from the haystack.

It amused Dannifer to see this hulking man so gently stroking the small creatures. He said, "They're sure comin' along fine, Muley. They still on the tit?"

"Weanin' nicely," Muley said. "I sure do thank you for lettin' me have 'em, mister." He looked again at Cotterage, but since there seemed no harm in the man, Muley was content to have him stand there.

"Maybe those are the fellas we'd like to see," Dannifer said. "Know which way they headed?"

"I didn't care," Muley said. "They just left me a mess to clean up. Then pa took off. Comes time to work, he's got to go to town." He scratched his head. "Funny you fellas didn't see him along the road."

"We must have been skylarkin'," Dannifer said. "Muley, did your pa say anything to you about some trouble here? It all happened when you went to Salem with the wagon."

Muley thought a minute, then shook his head. "He sure didn't mention it. What happened?"

"Well, it doesn't matter," Dannifer said. "I guess we'll go on back to Salem. Maybe we'll meet your pa on the road."

"If he shows up, I'll mention you was here," Muley said.

"I wouldn't," Dannifer advised. He winked. "We've got to keep something between ourselves, haven't we, Muley?"

It pleased Muley to be taken into confidence, and the men mounted up and rode out. At the road Dannifer looked back, and Muley Shotten waved.

Cotterage said, "Now what the hell did that settle?"

"The old man must have heard us on the road and ducked into the woods," Dannifer said. "Muley's too simple to think of lying. Whatever the old man's been up to, Muley don't know it's been going on."

"Damn it!" Cotterage said. "I hate a cold trail."

"It's the old man I want to see," Dannifer said. "I will, too, in time."

"When you do," Cotterage said, "you be sure and bring him to the law to deal with. People have got to stop handling these things themselves."

He rode along studying the grass along the road. The day was warm, but it was only bright-sun warm, not summer-season warm. On the higher peaks of the Cascades, snow crept downward, a visible barometer of approaching winter.

At the McCain place they both turned into the yard and dismounted. Angus McCain came out carrying his rifle. He took care to point it at no one, but he had it, and the threat was there.

"My woman don't want her to go," he said.

"How are you going to keep her?" Dannifer asked. "Locked up?"

"If I have to," McCain said. "It's what my woman wants."

Dannifer handed the reins of his horse to Cotterage and stepped toward McCain, who tightened his muscles a little, but made no further move. "Man, you don't want to shoot me. I saved her life, and you know that. You don't want to shoot me at all. Already you shot too quick, and now you're sorry for it. Do you want to do that again?"

He watched McCain, then reached out and took the rifle from him with no effort at all. Cotterage stepped up and took it from Dannifer, who went into the house. Mrs. McCain stood just inside the door, her hands pressed together, and when she saw Dannifer her eyes widened in surprise. Then she turned and ran to a door at the side and tried to block it with her body.

Angus McCain stepped into the cabin and said, "Let him pass, woman."

"I won't!"

He shook his head. "Are you goin' to keep her locked up? She'll hate us both. Let him pass, or I'll put you out of the way myself."

She gave no indication of obeying for a moment, then her defiance crumbled and she buried her face in tears in her apron. Dannifer stepped to the door and slid the bolt back. Tammy got up from the bed and picked up a canvas traveling bag and a blanket-wrapped bundle.

At the door she set them down and turned to her mother and touched her shoulder; Mrs. McCain jerked away and stood out of reach. "Go!" she yelled. "Go with the first pair of pants that comes through the hollow! Don't you think I know why you're so set on goin'? You've been together already. Go on, take up with him. I'll have no more to do with you!"

Angus McCain said, "She doesn't mean that, honey."

"I mean it! I mean it!" Mrs. McCain screamed. "I raised her to marry a man with a town house and a carriage and live like a fine lady! I wanted people to point with pride to her, and with pride to me." She wrung her hands in angry desperation. "I wanted her to be well fixed so I can be taken care of when I'm old and can't do for myself!"

Tammy said, "I didn't know you wanted to sell me, ma." Then she picked up her things and went out.

Cotterage followed and took the blanket bundle and made it fast to his saddle. Dannifer stepped out then and McCain was with him, walking a pace behind him. Dannifer helped

Tammy sit the horse sidesaddle, then he tied her canvas bag to the saddle horn and swung up beside her.

McCain said, "Don't hate her."

"It's hard to feel anything," Tammy said. "Would she come to town to see us when we get settled?"

"I don't know," he said honestly. "A pity she has to miss the weddin'." He looked at Pete Dannifer. "I don't know you, but I know my Tammy, and I think she's picked a better man than's grown around here. Would you do an old man a favor? Hold up the weddin' for two weeks, say two weeks from this comin' Sunday. Give me a chance to change her mind."

"That's a small enough thing for a man to do," Dannifer said, and Tammy hugged him. He grinned and reached down to shake McCain's hand. "I'll see you again." He nudged the horse into motion and they rode out of the yard.

Traveling along the town road, Elmer Cotterage kept studying the grass, and finally he pulled up and pointed. "Mule tracks. Left the road." He let his glance go up and out to the timber back from the road. "Shotten?"

"He has a ridin' mule," Tammy said.

"Shotten then," Cotterage said. "Heard us comin' and hid in the trees until we passed on." He sighed. "All right, we'll see him in Salem then. One place is as good as another to me."

Chapter 14

They reached town shortly after dark and went to the hotel; Early had left word with the clerk that they could use his two rooms, and Dannifer carried Tammy's things up the stairs. He opened the door, put her things down, and said, "Cotterage and I will share the room next door. I'd keep the door bolted, if I was you. This town can get wild on Saturday night."

He kissed her, and she said, "If the dining room is open, get a table. I'll be down as soon as I comb my hair."

"It looks all right to me."

"That's because you're a man," she said, and went in and closed the door.

He found Cotterage and Dan Holder in the lobby; both were wearing grave expressions. Cotterage said, "We can stop hunting for Shotten. Holder killed him earlier today. The damnedest thing, though. He came into the print shop and jumped him."

Holder nodded; he seemed to be on the edge of trembling, and he had liquor on his breath. Dannifer suspected that he was badly shaken up over the whole thing. "Shotten seemed enraged. I suppose it was the article in the paper; but damn it, the man couldn't read. Nearly everyone in town knows that." He shook his head. "I'm not a violent man, Dannifer. That blasted pistol I carry has been pure bluff. I never fired it but once before, until I put those bullets into Shotten's chest."

"Well, I'd keep on carrying it, if I was you," Cotterage said. He tapped Dannifer on the arm. "Do you suppose Neal Shute's up to some conversation?"

"We can go and see," Dannifer said.

"He hasn't left his store all day," Holder told them. "Say, could I go along? Somehow you're putting something together here that I don't know about."

Cotterage stroked his mustache. "I'm not sure what I'm after, but Shotten was mixed up with Romaine and his toughs somehow. After the killing at Wilkerson's place, Shute and a bunch went Indian hunting. Shute came back and McCain came back, and the bunch stopped off at Shotten's. Now where's the connection if any?"

"It is interesting," Holder said. "Well, I'll buy the supper, if we can find a table."

"That's the smartest thing you've said in the last ten minutes," Dannifer remarked, smiling.

They found a table and Dannifer went upstairs for Tammy. Cotterage had already ordered by the time he came back: fried ham, baked potatoes, and boiled cabbage. The ham was tasty enough, but the potatoes tasted like soap, and the cabbage had been cooked too long. Strong coffee helped, and there was a pie to top it off.

Pete Dannifer said, "What this town needs is a good restaurant, with someone who can cook more than one kind of meal a day."

"They'd get rich," Holder said.

Tammy looked up from her pie, and said, "Pete, loan me two hundred dollars."

He hesitated in surprise, then reached into his pocket and counted out the gold pieces. He was left with a twenty-dollar piece, which he carefully replaced. "Now, could I ask what you want two hundred dollars for?"

"I want to go to Portland on Monday's stage," she said. She leaned forward, a new excitement in her eyes. "The town *does* need another eating place. But I'd need a building. I don't suppose there's anything vacant along the street?"

She looked at Dan Holder. "You're around town all the time. Find me something." She motioned with her hands. "Something longer, or deeper, than it is wide. I'd want a long counter with benches, and just a few tables. It takes help to handle tables, but a counter saves walking." She laughed. "I learned that helping ma cook for harvest hands. Benches in a long row under the trees are easy to serve to. Tables are a bother."

"Well, I suppose I could come up with something," Holder said. He looked at Pete Dannifer, who was leaning back, an arm dangling. "You're going to be her husband. What do you think of a wife who runs a restaurant?"

"The idea interests me," Dannifer said. "Get the place, Dan. We'll work out the details when it shapes up." His glance touched Tammy. "I wouldn't go along with just a woman's whim."

"I wouldn't ask you to," she said. Then she reached across the table and took his hand. "Pete, maybe I'm testing you, or maybe I'm testing myself; it isn't really important which. But all my life I've lived in a house where man was supreme and woman was—well, just woman. It doesn't have to be that the life a man makes is for himself, and what happens to be left he gives to the woman. The trouble with Salem is that there's no competition. Shute's got the one store; and this hotel— I don't think they've ever served a good meal. Someday it may even have two newspapers."

"Oh, I'll like that," Holder said. "What are you going to buy in Portland with the two hundred dollars, Tammy?"

"A good stove with an oven, some dishes—just things I'll need."

"You could buy that at Shute's—" Holder said, then stopped and smiled. "Oh, I see. You're going to buy direct out of Portland, have Early freight it here, and cut out Shute's fat profit."

"Don't you think that's wise?" Tammy asked. "The man just can't take two cents out of every nickel that goes through Salem."

Dannifer said, "I'd feel a lot better about this if you'd gone to Portland with the half of Early's outfit that went back, rather than take the mail stage. Nobody's located those toughs of Shute's or the bunch Romaine had camped along the river. And if there's Indian trouble brewing—"

"The stage is heavily guarded," Tammy said. "Pete, now don't worry."

"That's easy to say and hard to do," Dannifer said. He got up, and Cotterage did the same. "If we're going over to Shute's store—"

"I was about to suggest it," Cotterage said. "Holder, why don't you take Miss McCain back to her room?"

"And miss this?" He laughed and shook his head. "Any girl who can go to Portland on the stage can find her way up a flight of stairs."

"You're quite right," Tammy said.

Cotterage paid for the meal and they went out to the street. Salem's saloons were lighted and gay, and the traffic was getting thick. Holder said, "The town's like a loose woman painting herself for the first performance of the evening." He let his glance travel up and down the street. "It's the momentary pleasures in life that count, gents." Then he added, "I'll bet no one has thought to find us another doctor."

"Wait until someone gets sick," Dannifer said, and led the way down the street to Neal Shute's store. Two clerks waited on the customers and one checked the day's receipts; he looked up when Dannifer approached the counter, and when he saw Holder and Elmer Cotterage he put down his pencil and came over.

"You're the Portland marshal," he said. "Heard you were in town. Saw you once or twice when I was there on business for Mr. Shute. What can I do for you?"

"We'd like to talk to Mr. Shute," Cotterage said.

"Gentlemen, I'm sorry, but Mr. Shute is resting." He glanced at Pete Dannifer and gnawed at his lower lip. "Perhaps tomorrow—"

"We'd like to see him tonight," Dannifer said politely. He looked around the store, at the bolts of cloth and hanging farm tools; the grocery department was at the rear and gave a spicy odor to the place. He saw the glass showcases, glanced at them casually; then his attention focused solidly on the gun case and he went over to it.

"Let me see that Colt's pistol there," he said.

Cotterage frowned in impatience. "Can't that wait?"

"Just a minute," Dannifer said. "Well, let me see it."

The clerk opened the case and took out the pistol and laid it on the glass top. Dannifer did not touch it or pick it up. He said, "It's not new. Where did you get it?"

"Mr. Shute put it in the case personally," the clerk said. "Beyond that, I know nothing about it."

"Then let me tell you something about it," Dannifer said. "Inside the grips, you will find the initials PD. On the loading lever, just behind the catch, you'll find a nick in the metal." He reached out and picked up the pistol and put it in his belt. "This is my property, and I thank you for finding it for me. I left this with the doctor and Wilkerson before I left Wilkerson's cabin, and I guess Mr. Shute will be glad to explain how he got it."

"You—you can't take that without paying for it!"

"Friend, I already paid for it once." The man opened his mouth to protest, but Dannifer held up his hand. "You can't sell something that don't belong to you in the first place."

"Well, I'm certainly going to tell Mr. Shute about this," the man said, and hurried into the back room. In a moment Cotterage nodded and they followed him. Holder reached the door first and opened it; the clerk turned his head around quickly and stopped talking.

Shute was sitting in a chair. He said, "Get out, and close the door, Hardison." Then he motioned for them to sit down, but he kept looking at Pete Dannifer through the puffed lids of his eyes. "You like the way I look?"

"I don't give a damn how you look," Dannifer said flatly. "You got what you wanted. Be happy with it."

"My face will heal," Shute said. "Then we'll have our fight good and proper. You won't surprise me the next time." His glance went to Cotterage. "What the hell do you want in Salem? Ain't you got enough trouble in Portland?"

"I'm looking for some friends of yours," Cotterage said. "Romaine's dead, so we can forget about him. But the rest of his kin has disappeared. That makes me nervous."

"You're the nervous kind," Shute said. "Everybody's nervous these days."

Cotterage sat down and leaned his elbows on his knees. "Where did you get the men to ride on the Indians?"

"In town. Where else?"

"Where are they now?"

"How do I know?" Shute said. "You pick up men like that, then never see them again."

"Not if they work around here," Holder said.

Neal Shute shrugged. "They must have got scared and lit out. I can't say as I blame them. McCain went crazy, I tell you. He just up and shot Two Bear, and then all hell broke loose. There wasn't anything to do but defend ourselves." He made an angry, cutting gesture with his hand. "You've got your guts, comin' here and blaming me. Holder, I asked you if you'd ride with me and you said no, and I asked Ted McGee and a dozen men in this town and they all said no. All right, so I took along some men who went for the money. By God, you ought to be thankful we got that kind of men." He stopped talking then and looked at Pete Dannifer's belt, looked at the pistol there. "Say, ain't—"

"Yes," Dannifer said. "Where did you get it?"

"In Two Bear's village," Shute said. "I found it. It's mine."

"No, it's mine. I just found it back."

"You can't steal from me," Shute said flatly. "I put a thing in my store, then it's for sale. I've whipped men for stealing crackers and cheese."

Dannifer grinned. "You do what you damn please. I don't care." Shute swung his feet to the floor and stood up. "Dannifer, I came to this country with a few dollars, a lot of ambition, and guts enough to make a go of it when other men failed. Things go my way around here because I want it that way. When a man challenges me, or my authority, I have to settle it so that there's no doubt as to who's in charge." He swung his glance to Elmer Cotterage. "If you've got Indian trouble, then bring in the army."

"I'd like to stop it without calling on the army," Cotterage said. "Besides, it would take them nearly two months to march here from the Presidio at San Francisco. Maybe you know the Territorial Governor, but—"

"I do know him," Shute interrupted. "Let me handle this."

"A little late for that," Dan Holder said mildly. "The Indians could burn and pillage half the valley by the time army action was taken. We've got to make peace with them. Where can we find the toughs you rode with, Shute?"

"I can't tell you, because I don't know," Shute said.

"We're not going to get anywhere," Cotterage said, turning to the door. The others moved with him, and Cotterage added, "Shute, you may be the biggest bear in this lick, but this badge makes me bigger than you. If I have to hang you to stop this Indian trouble, I will."

"You don't own a rope that'll hold me," Shute said. "Now get out of here."

They went out and Shute sat down and lit a cigar and smoked it while he thought this over. The damned marshal ought to stay in Portland where he belonged.

It was, Shute decided, time to back off and let the whole business take its course; he had given the Indians a push, and they'd raise hell before they were finally put down. And it would all take time and men, and while they were trying to save their little farms he'd get his saw camp set up and wait for the army contracts.

Shute didn't doubt that the army would be called in; all this followed a pattern that he had observed before. And the men who were ready for it made the money. He was troubled by Pete Dannifer, not so much because he was interfering, but because of the way he was doing it. Shute had seen his share of itinerant toughs; they were all cocky and full of trouble, but they were always a little in awe of power and position. He had expected Dannifer to be the same way, and had been surprised. Shute had his own impression of Dannifer, and it worried him, for the man seemed to act as though he could buy and sell Shute out of his pocket money.

A knock rattled the back door of his room and he went to it and opened it a crack. Shute said, "Come on in, Abe. The marshal's looking for you."

"Let him look," Abe said, and went immediately to the dresser and the whiskey bottle. He poured his drink. "We need some supplies."

"Who's with you?"

"I came alone with a pack horse," Abe said. "He's tied in the alley."

"Take what you want," Shute said. "Where have you been?"

"Some miles north," Abe said. "The Indians are raising hell, burning and killing. Three families were wiped out before we left. We decided to hightail it."

"You'd better not be seen in town," Shute said.

"Don't intend to," Abe said. "Romaine's bunch kind of got the hell knocked out of 'em, didn't they?" He looked at Shute's battered face. "You didn't happen to run into the same guy, did you?"

"He's here in town, big as pie," Shute said. "And you stay clear of him. I'll take care of Dannifer myself."

"I stopped fighting your fights when you were ten years old," Abe said. "But I don't know about Romaine's cousins. After Dannifer and the girl got away on the river, they followed and sent a man out in a canoe. He never came back, and they never found him, either. That damned man can take care of himself, Neal."

"And I can take care of myself," Shute said, tapping his chest. He put a match to his dead cigar. "We'll work our way out of this, Abe. I bought the steam engine and it'll be shipped right away. When I set up the saw rig, I want you to run the whole operation for me. In the meantime, we've got to save these poor settlers from the Indians."

Abe looked at him a moment, then laughed. "Now that's a twist. We start it and—"

"No, no! McCain started it. Out intentions were peaceful, but he lost his head and fired the first shot. Now I imagine that after we put down this uprising and tell our side of the story, the upright citizens will take him out and hang him." He butted out his cigar. "I'll be ready to ride at dawn. Where can I meet you?"

"About five miles north of McCain's place," Abe said. "I'll have forty men ready. Still three dollars a day and grub?"

"You can get scoundrels for that," Shute said. "Always pay the going rate, Abe, and not a dime more."

"Fool around long enough," Abe said, "and you'll get us both hung." He turned to the door. "I'll get the supplies now." Then he laughed. "Sometimes it's hard to remember who I'm chasin', Neal. Like when Romaine's men hit the Wilkerson place, and then the Injuns stumbled onto it, I felt kind of funny ridin' after 'em, when all along I knew—"

"A man keeps what he knows to himself," Shute said. "I'll see you in the morning." Abe nodded and opened the door, and Shute's voice was softer. "Abe, it won't always be like this. But for now it's better that you stay—well, kind of behind things and out of sight."

"I understand," Abe said, and closed the door behind him.

Dan Holder, who made a business of seeing and hearing everything that went on in Salem, did not discover that Neal Shute had left town until four days after he had gone, so quiet was Shute's departure. And Holder didn't know what to make of it; he knew that Shute had not taken the Portland mail stage; he had seen it off, for Tammy McCain and Elmer Cotterage had taken it.

Pete Dannifer was working a full crew of men at Ted McGee's place, setting up a sawmill, and the town was buzzing with talk about that. Holder found Dannifer there.

"Shute left town four days ago," Holder said. "What do you make of it?"

"He'll be back," Dannifer said. "Maybe he went to Portland."

"Why didn't he take the stage then?"

"Maybe he likes to ride," Dannifer said. "Dan, how do I know? And to tell you the truth, I care less. Tammy will be back in three days. Did you find that place for her?"

Holder nodded. "See Huber at the bank. He holds a lien against it for five hundred dollars. McGee and Jake Early ought to be in San Francisco by now." He looked at the sheds going up, and the bed to feed the saw, and said, "Be a shame if McGee couldn't buy the engine."

"He'll get it," Dannifer said.

"A very positive attitude," Holder admitted wryly. He took out his watch. "I believe it's time for my rye whiskey. Will I see you at the hotel this evening?"

"Well after dark," Dannifer said.

Holder went away and Dannifer went back to work. The sun was down and it was almost dusk when he sent the men home. He washed up at the spring, changed his shirt, and was getting ready to leave when he saw Angus McCain walking toward him, his step firm and determined.

McCain nodded. "I've been to the hotel. The clerk says my daughter left town, took the stage to Portland. I can't believe this."

"You'd better, because she did," Dannifer said.

A puzzled scowl showed on McCain's face. "My wife and I came to town to see her, to ask her to change her mind. Man, it was in your care that we left her. Perhaps you can explain to me why she went to Portland alone."

"To buy a stove."

"There's no sense to that. She could buy a stove from Shute."

"She didn't want to do business with Shute," Dannifer said. "His prices are too high."

McCain waved his hand. "I'm not makin' myself clear. It's not what she went for that bothers me, but that you let her go alone."

"There were seven passengers on the stage. Can't hardly call that alone, can you?"

"Strangers? You're twisting what I say."

"The Portland marshal was on the stage. He wasn't a stranger," Dannifer said. He reached out and tapped McCain on the chest. "Do you want to know somethin'? No, I can see that you don't. You want to go on your own pig-headed way, blind to everything but your own way of thinkin'. All right, go."

"I'm her father, and you answer to me," McCain said.

Dannifer said, "Look at me. Look hard at me. Now, how far do you think you can push me? Make up your mind now and do what you want to do."

For a moment McCain did not speak, then he said, "It bothers me. We wanted to give her away to a proper man, not have her taken from us."

"She wasn't yours to give," Dannifer said flatly. "I'm goin' to the hotel for supper. You and your wife want to join me there?"

"I guess not," McCain said, and stood there while Dannifer went on to town.

Chapter 15

Neal Shute and his private army had their first brush with Running Horse at the confluence of Ash Creek and the Clackamas River, and although Shute's men surprised the Indians, the battle turned sharply and he found himself all but surrounded, with his back against the river, and fighting for his life.

What Shute had first reckoned to be the Indian's main force of twenty or thirty warriors had turned out to be only the advance scouts, and after the shooting started, Running Horse brought up his reinforcements of more than a hundred braves.

Shute split his command, taking half and giving Abe fifteen men, and they dug in. Using their rifle butts, they tried to hold off the push of the main battle party. The Indians were armed with bows and arrows and a scatter of trade mus-

kets, and after the first attack Neal Shute wondered what all
the fuss was over letting the Indians have firearms. The arrows were more accurate and dangerous, by far, and could be
fired four arrows to one ball from the rifles of the defenders.
The muskets were not accurate at all.

Two of his men were wounded, both with arrows; no one
was hit by a ball from the trade muskets, although the Indians who had them did a lot of shooting. A few Indians died
in the fight and some were wounded and quickly carried
away. In the early afternoon, Running Horse pulled his men
back, and Shute and his fighters took to the river and drifted
with it toward the west.

A few miles from where they had entered the water, they
took to the south bank and mounted up and rode west. As
they moved along, Abe rode forward and they talked.

"Who got licked?" Abe asked.

"We didn't win," Shute said. He pointed ahead. "There's a
place about six miles from here where the stage stops. We'll
camp near there tonight, water up, and go back in the morning."

"I don't think anyone wants to get licked again," Abe said.
"We've got two men that ought to see a doctor."

"What doctor?" Shute asked. He reached out and tapped
Abe on the arm. "The next time I see those Indians, the outcome's going to be different."

Daylight was nearly gone when they reached the clearing
and the road and saw the lights of the settlement ahead.
Shute dismounted and the others followed him. The horses
were picketed well back in the trees, and the main camp was
made even further back, where the fires would not be visible
at the settlement.

Shute called Abe over. "I'll take those two wounded men
into the station and see that they're taken care of. Keep the
others here." He walked over to where the wounded men
were stretched out. One had a lung wound and wouldn't last;
the other had a broken arm. "You're going to have to sit a
horse for a spell," Shute told them. "I'll take you into the settlement ahead. We're three travelers who were jumped.
That's the only story you have. They'll take care of you."

Horses were brought up and the men hoisted on them, and
Shute mounted his own horse and led them out. As they approached the settlement he "hallooed" it and a man came out
with his rifle. He noticed then that the mail stage was stand-

ing by the shed, and a few passengers left the supper table to see who was coming.

Shute had never stopped here, so he had no concern about being recognized. He said, "We ran into Indians. My two partners are in bad shape."

"Let's get 'em inside," the man said. "You're in luck. A doctor's inside, goin' to Salem on the southbound stage."

Shute helped the lung-shot man off his horse and one of the passengers gave him a hand and they took him inside. They put him on two benches and the doctor brought his medicine bag; he was a skinny, serious man in his early thirties.

Everyone crowded around and Shute stepped back and looked around the room. He saw the woman sitting with her back to him, and he looked at her, feeling a tug of familiarity; then she turned her head and looked at him, no surprise at all in her expression.

"Are they your friends, Neal?" Tammy McCain asked. She got up and came over to him. "I've seen one of them before. Only he was a gypsy standing alongside the road to the Wilkerson place."

"What are you doing here, Tammy?"

"I've been to Portland. Could I ask the same question of you?"

He smiled. "Let's step outside where we can talk."

She hesitated, then shrugged and went out ahead of him. Full darkness had fallen, and away from the door and the light coming from it were solid, inky shadows. Shute said, "I guess this looks bad to you."

"Yes," she said. "What are you up to, Neal?"

"You wouldn't understand," he said. "I didn't expect to see you here."

"You did look surprised," she said.

"I can't let you go back in there," he said.

He spoke quietly, yet she was alarmed and tried to break past him for the door, but he quickly clamped a hand around her arm and another over her mouth and he roughly hauled her off. He was strong, and he mounted with her kicking and trying to scratch him; when he rode away, the owner of the settlement came running out, but Shute was clear of the yard and out of sight.

Chapter 16

The Portland mail stage was a day and a half late, and Pete Dannifer left firm instructions with the agent to notify him the moment it came in. He worked with worry looming larger and larger in his mind, and the work helped, for he drove himself and his crew hard. All the sheds were finished and the saw carriage completed, and the stone mortar work for the engine bed would be finished in three more days.

A man came from the express office in mid-afternoon, and when Dannifer saw him walking toward the saw camp, he put his maul and sack of nails down and went to meet him.

"Stage got in," the man said, and Dannifer outdistanced him to the main street. There was a crowd around the stage and in front of the office, and he made his way through, gently but firmly moving men aside. The agent was talking to a slender man in a brown suit, and he stopped when Dannifer came up. There was no Tammy McCain in sight.

"This is Doctor Simmons," the agent said. "Pete Dannifer."

"My pleasure," the doctor said, shaking hands.

"Where is Miss McCain?" Dannifer said abruptly.

"I was just telling the agent what happened, or as much as I know happened."

"Tell me," Dannifer said. His voice was quiet and tense.

"A man brought in two friends who had been wounded by Indians," Simmons said. "I took arrows out of both of them, but one died. No saving him. Got him right in the sternum, punctured the lower—"

"Never mind that," the agent said.

"Yes, of course," Simmons said. Dannifer's expression was frightening. "There were six passengers on the stage. Four businessmen looking for opportunity, Miss McCain, and myself. Frankly, I was quite occupied with the wounded men and paid little attention to what went on at the station."

"Which station?" Dannifer asked.

"Cassidy's, near the Clackamas," the agent answered.

"Go on," Dannifer said to the doctor, and he listened with a hard, stunned look on his face.

"Well, I can't say when Miss McCain and the stranger disappeared, but when I had finished my work, she was not in the station." He glanced about him. "For a time I thought she'd gone to the—ah—backhouse, but when she didn't return, I mentioned this to the proprietor. He looked for her and couldn't find her. Then we all looked. Both were gone."

"How much time had gone by?" Dannifer asked.

Simmons thought a moment. "I would judge better than an hour."

"Describe the stranger," Dannifer said.

"He was tall, as tall as you, but heavier. More muscular. His hair was dark and he had the beginning of a beard. Oh, yes—I noticed particularly his face. Badly bruised and cut. A fight, I'd say."

"Neal Shute," Dannifer said flatly. "Tammy wouldn't go with him of her own free will."

"Well, he was pretty sweet on her," the agent said.

He waved his arms at the crowd. "All right, folks, let's get on about our business. Make way there. Let the doctor through."

Dannifer stood still for a moment, then turned and saw Dan Holder at the edge of the crowd. Holder motioned to Dannifer and they went together to Holder's print shop. After Holder closed the door he said, "I wouldn't be surprised if we got snow in the valley before the week is out. Notice how it's been overcast and the weather's turned nippy?" He saw the expression on Dannifer's face and shook his head. "I don't know what Shute is up to either, but it's no good."

"She wouldn't go with him unless she was forced," Dannifer said again. "Dan, I'm going to kill that man."

"I figured that," Holder said. "And I'll be smiling when I write his obituary." He motioned toward a chair, then hurriedly took a pile of papers off it so Dannifer could sit down. "Pete, I don't want you running off half-cocked now. We've all got to sit tight and wait for Shute to make his move. For the life of me, I can't figure why he'd make off with her."

"Their meeting at the station must have been pure chance," Dannifer said. "And taking her with him must have been a sudden idea that just came to him." He gnawed his lip. "Everyone on the stage except Tammy was a stranger to Shute. Was it because she recognized him?"

"We've got to wait," Holder said. "That's the hardest part, Pete." He reached out and slapped Dannifer on the shoulder. "Go on back to your camp. I'll keep an eye on the town for you."

"You're right," Dannifer said. "With my head I know you're right, but it's not what I want to do." He got up and went to the door. "My pistol's at camp. I'm goin' to start wearin' it. When Shute comes back, I'm goin' to shoot him."

He walked slowly back to the saw camp and climbed onto the roof of the saw shed and started laying shingles. He worked until dark; then he washed and went to the hotel for his supper. Holder was there and they ate together, but they didn't talk much. They were having their coffee when Angus McCain came in and saw them, and came to the table, sitting down without waiting for an invitation.

"Neal Shute sent me word," McCain said dully. "He has my little girl." He looked at Dannifer as though waiting for him to be surprised. "Well, man, doesn't it mean anythin' to you at all?"

"I knew Shute had her," Dannifer said. "Damn it, what does he want?"

"Me," McCain said. "He sent a man with word that I was to ride to the Clackamas. I'd be met there. Shute's making a deal with the Indians. He's to give me up to them to be punished for starting the war. If I don't come, I've lost my little girl."

Dan Holder slapped the table. "By God, I see what he's doing. He's making a damned hero of himself. Why, if he stops the Indian trouble, everyone will kiss his muddy boots. And they won't care a damn how he did it."

"You came to me," Dannifer said to McCain. "Why? Because you want out of it?"

"A man wants to live, even with his conscience," McCain said. "No, I don't want to die. I thought I did, after what I went and done, but when it comes to the hard facts of it, a man wants to go on. Shute's got to be stopped. The man's no good. I always knew it."

"If you did, why didn't you do somethin' a long time ago?" Holder asked bluntly.

McCain looked at the knots in the table. "It was too much trouble. A man thinks of himself first; it's the kind of beast he is." He looked up at Dannifer. "I want to pay for what I done, Dannifer. But I'm human. I don't want to pay too much."

"But it is important that you pay, so you can sleep nights," Dannifer said.

"Aye," McCain said. "It's hell to be that way, but how can I change what I am?"

"I don't guess you can," Holder said. He looked at Pete Dannifer. "What are you thinking about? A way out?"

"There's got to be a way out," Dannifer said. He looked at McCain. "You're goin' through with this."

"Give myself up to Shute so he can turn me over to the Indians?"

"That's right," Dannifer said. "And you're goin' to hope I can get you out of there before they kill you."

"You want me to put a lot of faith in—"

"Forget it then!" Dannifer snapped. "I'll go my own way. To hell with you! Go on, get out of here!" He reached out and gave McCain a push. "You hear me! Get out of my sight!"

McCain stood up slowly. He stared at Dannifer. "What kind of a man are you who'd let the father of the woman he means to marry—"

Dannifer reared erect. "I said, get out!"

For a moment McCain hesitated, then he turned and hurried out. After he'd gone, Holder said, "I didn't think you'd do a thing like that, Pete."

"Oh, hell, I don't want him killed," Dannifer said. "He'd be like tits on a boar, useless if I took him with me." He leaned forward and spoke softly. "Dan, I need six or eight good men. You know the kind I want, who can sit a horse twenty hours straight, and walk sixty miles after the horse is gone."

"I can get them for you," Holder said. "And I regret that I'm not that kind of man myself. When do you want them?"

"Tonight," Dannifer said. "No fuss about this, Dan. Everything quiet. I want to trail McCain but I don't want him to know it."

"He might not—"

"He'll go," Dannifer said. "Crying all the way, but he'll go. The man has to do it, you see. It will absolve him in Tammy's eyes; he'd go out thinkin' that all her life she'll regard him as a hero."

"If you make a mistake and McCain is killed, you'll probably have the mother moved in with you," Holder said.

"I thought of that, and what stronger reason could a man have for keeping Angus McCain alive?" Dannifer said. "I'm going to leave the arrangements to you, Dan. Pick good horses, and see what you can do about getting hold of some repeating pistols, or Colt's revolving rifles."

"I'll take care of everything."

Dannifer went back to McGee's cabin and got his pistol and belt and checked the powder flask, shot pouch, and cap box. He rolled blankets, a skin sleeping robe, and some clothes, and left them outside against the cabin wall; then he walked back to the express office. The clerk was there, and Dannifer said, "Miss McCain was to make a few purchases for me in Portland. Were there any bundles on the stage?"

"Yes," the clerk said. "Her luggage too." He set three pieces on the counter. "If you'll just sign for them—"

Dannifer scrawled his name and took the things to the hotel. One was her traveling bag, and he put that on her bed and then unwrapped the two bundles. One contained clothes, a leather coat, and a heavy shirt; the other was wrapped in straw and he carefully opened it and took out a box made of polished cherry. He put this on the night stand by the lamp and opened it, and lifted out a new .44 Colt's pistol with detachable shoulder stock. He clamped the claw around the butt and tightened the screw, then shouldered the piece, trying it out for drop and lay against his cheek. The powder flask was in the butt, as well as a small cap box, and he filled both; after that he loaded the gun and went out, locking the door behind him.

At Dan Holder's office he found two men waiting. When he went in they looked at him and nodded, but said nothing. "Where's Dan?" he asked.

One shrugged. The other, a short, bull-necked man said, "Looking for six more men." Then he extended his hand. "I'm Regan. That's my blacksmith shop down at the end of the street. This is Osman."

They were, Dannifer noticed, heavily armed, with weapons that seemed quite familiar to them. Dannifer's distinction was his skill in observation; he had seen movers armed with pistols and they wore them awkwardly, uncomfortably, and you could tell that such men would rather put down the pistol and pick up an ax. These two men showed none of that. He did not question them about their experience; it would be sufficient.

Another man came in, a tall, slow-moving man. Dannifer had seen him about town but had never met him. "Name's

Thursday," he said. "Got no other. Foundling." He nodded to Osman and Regan. "Seems we're goin' on a little skunk hunt."

"Well, I never liked Shute anyway," Regan said.

Others came, four more, then Holder with the final man; he locked the front door and pulled the shades over the windows. "Gents, this is Pete Dannifer. Likely you know him, or have seen him around town."

"I seen him put Shute down," one said dryly. "That's recommend enough for me."

"Dan's probably told you what's going on," Dannifer said, and they all nodded. "Shute wants to put down the Indian trouble and make a hero out of himself. With the girl, he'll force McCain to give himself up and get killed. Maybe it'll satisfy the Indians and maybe it won't. It ain't the Indians I mean to satisfy. They never come out too good anyway when they mix it up with white men. But we've got to get the girl away from Shute. She's his hole card."

"Then let's get at it," Regan said.

Dannifer looked at Holder. "When can you have the horses ready?"

"In an hour. In back of the stable."

"We'll meet there," Dannifer said. "And I want to thank you for coming. Shute's not alone. He must have twenty men with him, all hardcases."

"Those odds suit us," Regan said. "Let's go get a drink."

They went out and Holder locked the door again; he lit a cigar and sat down at his littered desk. Finally he said, "I suppose you'll kill Shute when you find him."

"That's a good guess."

"It's too bad."

Dannifer looked at him in surprise. "Why?"

"Well, I suppose because these people have got to learn to enact their own punishments. You see, a man usually takes care of his own trouble. Pretty soon people get to saying, ' "Well, So-an-so will take care of it," ' and before you know it, one man's running it all. People have got to sit on juries and try men—not man against man, but communities against man."

"So what am I supposed to do?"

"Bring Shute back alive. Kicking and squealing like a pig."

"That's asking a lot," Dannifer said.

Holder shrugged. "It's always harder to do right than it is to do wrong. Think about it?"

"I can do that," Dannifer admitted. Then he turned to the door. "Let's you and me get a drink."

Chapter 17

Neal Shute and Abe camped together; they had built their fires against the creek, and were surrounded on all sides by dense woods. Then Shute left his fire and walked over to where Tammy McCain sat. Her ankles were tied, but her hands had been freed so that she could eat her supper; a man squatted fifteen feet away, watching her.

When Shute waved his hand, the man got up and moved away and Shute sat down. "I'll have to tie your hands again, Tammy. You won't let me trust you."

"Don't ever trust me, Neal," she said. "Don't ever let me get my hands on a gun or a knife or a hunk of wood when you're in reach."

"Do you hate me that much?"

"I don't hate you at all," she said. "I just know that you have to be stopped."

He laughed. "No one's goin' to do that, Tammy. I'm goin' to settle this Indian trouble, and people are goin' to be grateful to me."

"You took me by force," she said. "How do you intend to explain that?"

"I don't intend to explain at all," he said. "Who'll stand up to me? The town? They're too busy plantin' and fellin' timber and makin' money to risk anything. And if you're thinkin' of Dannifer, then you'd better look around you. When I go back, these men go with me. What kind of a chance would he have?"

"He's not afraid of you."

"No, I suppose not. Then I'll have to teach him fear," Shute said. "I'll have to teach you, too, Tammy."

"What could you teach me?"

He shrugged. "I've tried to reason with you. My patience

has an end. I could take you to my blanket without marriage. Dannifer's done that. Only my consideration——"

"You pig, you don't have any consideration!"

His heavy face took on a dark, brooding look. "When I've made terms with the Indians," he said, "you and I'll have to be alone for a spell. I've got a way with a woman, you know."

"Like a ruttin' stud!" she snapped.

He slapped her face hard enough to knock her down, then he stood up. "I could have my fun and pass you around to the men," he said. "What good would you be afterward? You think about that." He pointed to her plate. "Hurry up and eat your supper."

She felt like telling him the food was slop and she wanted none of it, but she held it back, realizing that if she was going to get out of this she'd have to use her head and not her temper.

So she picked up her plate and began to eat slowly, and Neal Shute turned away. The man who had been guarding her didn't come back at once, so she quickly ripped her petticoat into strips and wrapped her wrists heavily, then pulled her sleeves down and buttoned them. She had hardly finished when the guard came back.

He looked at her plate and said, "Didn't eat it all, huh? Too bad, lady. Now I've got to tie your hands."

She put her hands behind her and he snugged the rope tightly and checked the knot. Then he got up and joined the others at a fire twenty yards away. Tammy lay on the ground and waited until the camp settled down for the night, and she figured it was well after midnight before she dared work on the ropes binding her wrists. With her hands tied behind her, and fingers numb from the cold and lack of circulation, she had trouble finding an end to the cloth wrapping. But she kept at it, worked up a sweat over it, and finally pulled it loose a bit at a time. With one wrist fairly free, she quickly got the cloth loose from the other and gained enough slack in the rope to free one hand. Ten minutes later she had her ankles unbound and was rubbing them to get the circulation back.

No one had stirred for what must have been an hour, and she carefully inched away from the camp. Her first thought was to get a horse, but then she figured they'd have a guard posted; and even if there was none, she ran a risk of frightening the animals, raising an alarm.

She knew she'd have to escape afoot, and once her mind was made up on it she struck out for the river. She went for what she reckoned was a mile, then cut away from it. Shute would figure she'd make for the river, and she was sure she left a clear trail. Because she knew him to be a stubborn, opinionated man, she felt that he would go to the river, even if the trail was not distinct, or petered out completely.

Her shoes came off and she carried them; being barefoot slowed her down, but she would leave less of a trail, and her feet were sensitive and could feel a twig before she stepped on it and broke it. Her search was for rocky ground, and she stayed with it although the stones bruised her feet. There was no way of knowing whether or not Shute had discovered yet that she was gone; to be safe, she figured that he had, but for the last couple of hours she had been traveling on rocky ground and had left no sign, no hint of a trail.

Finally she had to rest, so she sat on a flat rock and got her breath and thought things over. Her mind kept going back to the time Pete Dannifer engineered their escape from Wilkerson's place; you had to keep thinking, no matter how tired you were; you had to outsmart the other man.

Tammy realized that she couldn't escape afoot by leading Shute on a chase. Her only chance lay in outsmarting him, and she figured she had done the right things by starting him on a blind trail, and then reversing her direction. This was rough country, hard for a horseman to travel, but it could be passed over more easily by a person afoot. Around her were citadels, high prominences where she could see for miles; it was an ideal place to hole up, and she figured this would have been the thing Pete Dannifer would have done.

The predawn cold was biting, and she tried to put her shoes back on, but she found her feet were pretty badly swollen; she had to pinch them into the shoes and leave the bottom four buttons unfastened.

Daylight came slowly and she waited impatiently for it. At last she could make out something of her surroundings, and she moved to another spot, a higher place beneath a rock overhang and protected on three sides. The view here was excellent, and she could even make out the distant slash in the trees that marked the course of the Clackamas; it was a good eight or nine miles as the crow travels, and a lot more than that for anyone making it on horseback.

She could also study her back trail, and she was surprised

to see how difficult it had been. Surely no horseman would try it, and this gave her a feeling of security.

Her hunger was something she couldn't do anything about, but she'd been hungry before and hadn't died from it. She was thirsty and that bothered her some; but it wasn't bad yet, and she had no intention of leaving this high rocky ground for at least another day.

She remained in that one place and the day warmed a little, in spite of the overcast; in the afternoon it started to snow, and as soon as the snow began to grow thick on the rocks she would scoop some off and melt it in her mouth. It solved her thirst problem, but presented another: she wouldn't be able to travel now without leaving tracks, though as long as it kept snowing and covered them up she'd be all right; but when it stopped she'd leave a trail as plain as a yell.

Now was the time to move, she figured, so she worked west, staying among the rocks. She finished out the day moving toward the Portland road and the settlement she knew was there. Darkness slowed her but she would not stop, for she had to take advantage of the falling snow. Throughout the night she forced herself to keep moving, and when it was near dawn she thought she must have traveled another eight or nine miles.

She found the road at last, and stopped to figure out which way she should go. A small creek bubbled nearby and she remembered the stage fording it just before arriving at the settlement, so she turned south and walked a ways until she came to it. The corral was crowded with horses and she had a moment of panic; she thought Shute was at the settlement with his bunch. Still, she had to do something. She couldn't go on in this cold without a heavier coat. And she had to have something to eat.

Indian-cautious, she approached the buildings, skirted them, and tried the back door. The bolt gave to her hand pressure and she eased it open and stopped, hearing the snores of sleeping men. Her nose told her that she was near the pantry, and she felt carefully along the wall until she touched shelves. She found some bread and a hanging hock of ham, and her hand went along another counter and stopped when she touched the rounded stock of a firearm. Quickly she felt of it and discovered that it was a pistol with a stock attached. She took it and made her way outside, closing the door soundlessly.

Her first instinct was to leave the yard, but she was held there against the wall by a nagging thought. She put the bread and ham down in the snow and tried to look more carefully at the gun, but it was too dark to see. So she explored it with her fingers, and pulled in her breath sharply when she felt the round cylinder. Quickly she felt of the stock, at the brass cap box there, and the powder-horn cap with the tiny brass chain dangling from it. She knew this weapon, for she had bought it herself.

She opened the door again, banging it loudly, and a man snorted in surprise and left his blankets, grabbing her around the ankles, tripping her.

"Get a light!" he yelled, and someone struck a flint against the rough edge of a tinder box.

The place came alive then and candles were lit, and Pete Dannifer stood there. He saw her and swore, and he then threw his arms around her.

"I was going to steal your gun," she said, and tried not to cry with relief. "Oh, my, the bread and ham! I left it outside in the snow."

The man who had grabbed her said, "Is this the McCain girl, Pete?"

Dannifer nodded. "Somebody stoke up the fire and put some coffee on." He led Tammy into the big room and prodded the coals in the fireplace, added wood, and soon had a fire blazing.

"How did you get away from Shute?" he asked.

She told him about wrapping her wrists to make them bigger, and he laughed. "When I saw the horses, I thought Shute was here," she said, "and that's why I sneaked in and stole the ham and bread and the gun."

Regan and Osman and the others were standing around, and Pete Dannifer looked at them. "Big Indian fighters," he said. They looked sheepishly at each other, then Osman smiled.

"It was your gun she stole," he said, and they all laughed.

Pete Dannifer grinned and scratched his head. "Now, you didn't have to mention that." He looked at Regan. "Go wake McCain."

"My father's here?" Tammy asked.

Regan turned and went into another room. "Shute was forcing him to turn himself over to the Indians," Dannifer said. "We trailed him for a day, then took him in tow." He glanced at the others as though to warn them to say nothing more, and the men stood silently.

McCain came out, stopped, then went to her and put his arms around her. He cried, and it embarrassed the men. Osman said, "A man ought to control himself better than that."

Another man said, "Shut up. It's not our business."

McCain got a grip on himself and wiped his eyes. "Thank God you're safe," he said. "I had faith that he'd release you, child. No man is that black."

"He didn't release her," Dannifer said. "She got away on her own."

McCain was stunned. "Why, I thought—" He looked at the others. "Why should I go on now?"

"Because I say you should," Dannifer said. "I want Shute and his gang, and I mean to have 'em. You're with us all the way, McCain. Understand that?"

"Against my will?"

"I've had enough of you," Thursday said. "You was high-tailin' it back when we caught you. Look at your girl, man. For once in your life face up to it. Look at her, and tell her you were goin' to let Shute have her."

He tried, but he couldn't meet Tammy's eyes; he buried his face in his hands and shook his head from side to side. "I didn't want to die," he said. "Hate me if you want to, but I just didn't want to die."

"I don't hate you, pa," Tammy said. "But I understand you better. You're goin' on, and whatever Pete asks you to do, you'll do."

"He wants me to ride into Shute's camp alone!"

"Then you'll do just that," she said. "Pa, you've always been a proud man, and I'm not goin' to discuss it now as to whether it's real pride or your own fanciful thinkin', but you're goin' to do what Pete wants, or by thunder I'll tell this all over town!"

He stared at her, then looked at the others. "What's to keep them from tellin'?"

"They ain't the kind who'll tell," she said firmly. "I'm goin' to ride along, pa. I'm goin' to be there to see that you do like a man would."

"Don't let her go," McCain said to Dannifer.

The Texan shook his head. "She can go if she wants to," he said, and turned to Tammy. "I guess between us we can

outfit you in man's clothes. You put your hair up inside a hat
and dirty your face a little, and we could pass you for a man.
If Shute ever sees you and recognizes you—"

"I understand," Tammy said. "And I think I could lead
you right to his camp."

"That's sure where we're goin', little lady," Thursday said.

"How many men does he have?" Regan asked.

"About thirty."

"Them odds suit me," Osman said. "Let's get some sleep. I
like to be in the saddle before dawn."

"That's just around the corner," Dannifer said. "Let's get
some hot mush in our bellies, and some sidemeat."

The others moved away, but Dannifer sat with McCain
and Tammy; she wanted to huddle near the fire and let the
heat soak her. "You had a time, huh?" Dannifer said.

"I made it," she said. "That's the important thing, ain't it?"

"Sure is. You stay close to me from now on."

"If she hadn't gone to Portland," McCain said, "none of
this—"

"Why don't you shut up, pa?" Tammy interrupted.

His jaw dropped in shock. "You can't talk to me that
way!"

"Can't I? Why not?" She looked steadily at him. "Pa, I
love you because you are my pa, but I ain't yours no more.
Do you understand that? I'm my own woman, Pete's woman.
Nothin's the same."

"Somebody ought to be to blame for this," McCain said.
"It just seems that somebody ought to."

"Blame for what?" Dannifer asked. "Friend, it ain't possible for a man to go through life without findin' out what he
really is. Sometimes the knowledge breaks a man so bad that
he just can't ever get up again. I've seen that. And I've seen it
where a man found out that bitter truth and lived with it, and
maybe was a little better because of it. It's something you've
got to face, McCain. You made a mistake, you and Shute.
Nothin' you can do or tell yourself is goin' to change that."

The meal was ready and they sat around the big table and
ate. Afterward Tammy took the borrowed clothes into the
root cellar and put them on. When she came back everyone
laughed at the poor fit, but they agreed that with some soot
on her face she'd pass for a small man.

"McCain, I want you to strike out for the Clackamas.
We'll be about half a mile behind you. Make contact with
Shute, then we'll hit him." He reached across the table and

took McCain's arm. "Man, if you give us away by any word or action—"

"You hurt me," McCain said, "and my daughter would never forgive you."

"He won't have to," Regan said. "We'll take care of you. And we wouldn't kill you, either. You can have your damned life, whatever you think it's worth."

McCain looked at them and said, "All my life I've been a farmer, a man of peace. The only violence I ever committed was against them Indians. Can't a man be forgiven for his mistake?"

"Too many people have already paid too much," Thursday said. He looked at Dannifer. "How are we goin' to take Shute? In an open fight, or cut and run?"

"It's my opinion," Dannifer said, "that most of Shute's men will scatter when the fight gets hot. You put 'em against men who can lick the pants off of 'em and they'll lose their stomach damned quick. Shute's a skinflint, and he can't pay much. That gold will look pretty small when the bullets come close." He tapped off a count on his first two fingers. "I want Neal Shute, and the one they call Abe. Ain't that what you said his name was, McCain?"

"He's Shute's left hand," McCain said.

"Those two I want," Dannifer said. "Alive if possible."

"Dead's easier," Thursday said.

"They're goin' back to Salem for trial," Dannifer said.

Osman laughed. "Who'll you get to try 'em?"

"We'll bring in a judge from Portland," Dannifer said. "Dan Holder is right; they're the town's responsibility, not ours alone. We're kind of like sheriffs with a posse. We catch 'em, and the town tries 'em."

"What about the Indians?" Regan asked. "They're still on the warpath."

"I don't know what we can do about that," Dannifer admitted. "Of all the Indians I've seen, they've come out the short end every time. In Texas we've been shootin' on sight for thirty years. I guess Kansas and the plains country ain't much better." He shook his head. "Maybe the only way to settle this is to fight an Indian war. Bring in the army and get it over with. Time's past, it seems like, to settle anything by talk. Neither side trusts the other."

"That's a hell of a state," Regan said.

"That's the way I felt," McCain said, "when that lyin' Injun told me he didn't have my girl."

"He was tellin' you the truth," Dannifer said. "I don't blame you for not believin' him. We get ourselves worked up over these things. The point is, we can't act in a hurry. That's why Shute and Abe have got to go back, be given time to let people cool off and think it over." He got up from the table and picked up his gun. "Let's get mounted up."

Chapter 18

The snow was still falling, a gentle, finely flaked snow, and dawn was a bleak grayness when they swung out of the yard and headed for the Clackamas River. McCain moved on ahead and soon pulled out of sight, and Dannifer kept the pace down so that McCain was always half a mile or more ahead.

They made a wide sweep during the morning to approach the Clackamas from the south, and Dannifer seemed to be in no particular hurry. He studied the tracks and the snowfall carefully; McCain's trail was barely visible. Once it became clearer and he called a halt. At first Tammy did not understand this, then she realized how Dannifer was judging his distance behind her father. If the tracks were nearly filled over, he was keeping his distance, but if they were not, it meant that he was gaining and should fall back a little.

When they came to the river, the sign was clear that McCain had met Shute. Tracks were everywhere, and Dannifer crossed his bunch at the exact spot Shute had used.

The trail swung to the northeast and Dannifer followed it, studying the tracks, knowing that he was gaining a little all the time. They were in dense timber, and finally he raised his hand and they stopped. Regan sniffed the air and said, "Lodge smoke."

"Dismount," Dannifer ordered. They picketed the horses and went forward on foot for half a mile, when they stopped again. In a small clearing, backed up against a creek, Shute was making camp, and Dannifer surmised that this was where he was going to meet the Indians.

Dannifer gestured outward with his hands and his men split up, silently encircling Shute's camp. Dannifer was picking his route in, and Tammy went with him. They had hardly cleared the trees when one of Shute's men spotted them and a dozen guns swung their way. Dannifer spoke softly. "We'll walk to the near side of that deadfall and stop. It's a good sixty yards from the camp. When I tell you, drop behind that log."

"All right," Tammy said. Then she added, "If I ain't too scared to move."

"Then I'll push you."

When they drew near the log, Neal Shute recognized Dannifer, and he yelled, "That's far enough! I've got McCain here! I don't need you!"

"Not too late to give it up," Dannifer said. "Get out with a whole skin."

"You can't bargain with me," Shute said. He stopped speaking while Abe came up and said something softly to him. Shute looked around. "Where's your bunch? Or couldn't you get one together?"

Dannifer didn't answer him. "McCain, come here!" he called.

"He stays!" Shute yelled. "I've got the girl!" He pointed to the fire sending up smoke. "By morning the Indians will be here. We're goin' to palaver and I'm goin' to make a trade. You ain't going to stop it, Dannifer, because McCain's going to do what I say. If he don't, I'll kill the girl."

"The liar," Tammy said, and whipped off her hat, letting her long hair fly loose. "How are you going to do that, Neal?" she yelled.

Dannifer stiff-armed her and sent her sprawling behind the deadfall, and he hit the ground himself as the bullets thudded into the log. He peered around one end, the snout of his pistol pointed in the right direction, and he coolly dropped a man standing near Shute.

From around the camp, rifles cracked and men scattered, firing as they ran. McCain broke away from the men holding him, seized a rifle, and shot a man before going down. Shute and Abe took cover behind a heavy fallen branch, and fired from that position, while from the fringe of the camp accurate rifle-shooting thinned out the number of Shute's men. Six were down, and the rest broke for the horses, but two more fell before they could mount up.

Dannifer shouted, "Drive them on, Regan! Keep drivin' 'em!"

He saw three men dart from tree to tree, shooting, loading,

and shooting again; they followed the mounted men, pushing them to the north, away from Shute's camp.

Only two remained, the two Pete Dannifer wanted, and he yelled for the shooting to stop. "Shute? Listen to me! We're all around you! Do you want to die now, or take your chance at a trial in town?"

For a moment there was no answer at all; then Shute said, "I'll take my chances in town. Does that deal go for Abe too?"

"Both of you," Dannifer said. "Throw out your guns and stand up with your arms raised."

They obeyed him, and Thursday and the others left the trees and took charge of the camp. One of the men, named Perry, looked around to see if anyone else was alive. Then he called, "Pete! McCain's been shot through the hip!"

Leaving his cover from behind the deadfall, Dannifer and Tammy went into the camp. The two prisoners were being tied, Indian style, with stout poles under the arms and running across their backs. McCain was being raised to a sitting position and he cried out in pain.

"The bullet's got to come out," Perry said.

Dannifer nodded in agreement. "Can you do it?"

"I have done it before," Perry admitted. "We ought to get him drunk first."

"There's no time for that. Get someone to hold him down, or knock him out." Dannifer looked at the sky and judged how much of the afternoon was left. The snow was lessening and that pleased him, but he was surprised to find that little else did. McCain would have to stand in the prisoner's dock with Neal Shute and Abe.

Dannifer walked over to the two prisoners. Shute stared at him, then smiled. "Dannifer, I'll get you yet."

"Why don't you shut up?" Abe said sullenly. "I told you you'd end up gettin' us hung."

"We're a long way from the rope," Shute said. "Abe worries a lot."

"He has a right to," Dannifer said, and looked from one to the other. "Are you two related, by any chance? There's a resemblance."

"We're brothers," Abe said. He turned his head and looked at the men near the fire. McCain was on the ground, a blanket having been spread, and Perry was kneeling by him while two others held him down.

"The cold will help stop the bleedin'," Abe said. "I went

through that once." Then he lost interest in what they were doing, and glanced at Tammy McCain. "We chased all over hell and back tryin' to find you. How did you get away?"

"What difference does it make now?" Neal Shute said. He was silent for a moment, then snapped his head around; they all did that, for they could hear a volley of shots, then another, ragged and hurried.

They listened for more shooting but none came. Just then McCain screamed and someone cracked him on the jaw and the screaming stopped. Perry swore a little as he worked. Tammy turned away, for this was brutal business and she didn't want to watch. In a little while it was over and they were binding McCain's wound and making a litter for him.

Regan ran out from the fringe of the woods, his men with him, and now and then they looked behind them as they ran toward the fire. Regan was out of breath, and he stood there, legs spread, panting heavily. "Ran—better'n a—mile. Injuns —about a hundred—right behind us." He wiped his hand across his mouth and took several deep breaths. "We pushed that bunch right into 'em, Pete. Not a man got out of it. Not one."

"We may have to make a fight of it here," Dannifer said. "No time to run." He waved them to what cover was available. "I don't want any shootin' until they attack us. You understand?"

Two men went out and brought the deadfall into the camp, and they dragged other pieces of logs and limbs to form a kind of boxlike cover.

"What about us?" Shute asked. "Are we goin' to stand up and get killed?"

"You ain't goin' to lick no hundred Indians," Abe said. "There's no chance but to run for it. Cut us loose."

Dannifer ignored him. He cocked his pistol and handed it to Tammy and said, "The mainspring is pretty stiff, so if you have to shoot and recock it, use both thumbs. If either of 'em tries to break, break a leg."

"I will," she said, and pointed the gun at Neal Shute.

"Heads up," Thursday said, and looked toward the trees.

The Indians appeared, a nearly solid line of them, and Dannifer saw that his party was ringed, cut off completely. While the main body of Indians remained at the fringe of the clearing, a group of six advanced.

"Anyone speak their talk?" Dannifer asked without raising his voice.

"I do," Shute said.

"You keep your mouth shut," Dannifer told him. "How about you, Regan? You lived with 'em."

"I can get along with it," Regan said.

"Let's go meet 'em then," Dannifer said, and he and Regan went forward, stopping halfway between the camp and the trees.

The Indians looked them over carefully, then one spoke at length. When he was through, Regan said, "He says we're cut off and outnumbered. He will kill us as he killed the others."

"Ask him if he will talk of peace instead of war," Dannifer said. This was relayed, and Regan listened to the answer.

"His name is Running Horse, and he is the leader of his people," Regan said. "He has no love for war, but war was put on him by white men. The winter is here and there will not be enough food because of war. He will talk peace if it's a true peace."

"Tell him he has just killed the last of the men who raided Tanan Two Bear's camp. Tell him he has had his revenge, and that we have as our prisoners men who would have liked to see the Indians go on fighting until the army came and killed them, or moved them to another land far away. Tell him that our food is theirs; it will take them to their lodges. Tell him there is no more need of war."

Regan talked for a time, then said, "He wants to know what will happen to them because of the homes they burned. Will the white man now want war?"

"Tell him it is done and over," Dannifer said. "Only more men would die, and enough have died already. He is welcome to our food. We'll go our way and he can go his."

This was related to the Indians, Regan embellishing it a little. Then he listened to Running Horse speak, and translated it for Dannifer.

"He says they would all like to go home, but since they are already here and we can't escape, why not kill us and then go home?"

Dannifer thought about that, and said, "Tell him that we are not women who will give up without a fight. Tell him that if it is to be war we will die now, but he will die with us, and perhaps thirty of his braves. Ask him if that will help feed them this winter? He can take food and they can go home with full bellies; or he can die here, along with many of his men, and there will be a new chief."

Regan put that argument to them, and it impressed Running Horse. He talked it over with his medicine man, then agreed that Dannifer's argument was good. They would take the food and go, and Dannifer nodded for Regan to give them everything they had. No one protested. Neal and Abe Shute stood silently under the pistol Tammy McCain held, and the Indians took all their stores and left the way they had come, going north toward their lodges.

"Let's break camp," Dannifer said. "Thursday, rig a travois for McCain. We'll go back to the settlement along the road."

"What about horses for us?" Neal Shute asked. "They ran off all our—"

"Walkin' won't hurt you any," Regan said.

In half an hour they left the clearing and struck out for the Portland road. Tammy rode double with Dannifer, for they needed her horse for the travois. The snow was a foot deep, deep enough to make hard work out of walking, and Regan had no sympathy at all; he put the Shute brothers to work breaking trail.

And they broke trail until they reached the settlement.

It was late, well past midnight when they arrived, and the owner got up and built a fire and they carried McCain in and put him to bed. He was in pain, and after Dannifer and Tammy had had coffee they went in to see the wounded man.

McCain's face was drawn and pale; the room was cold and the covers were pulled to his chin. A lamp burned by his bedside. "I killed one," he said. "Dannifer, I was ready to die if I could take one along." Then he looked at Tammy. "Don't be ashamed of me, child."

"I'm not ashamed of you, pa."

"That's good," he said. "And it's good to know you've paid."

"Maybe the payin' isn't over," Dannifer said. "We're takin' Neal Shute and Abe back to Salem to trial, and you know what he's goin' to say: that it was all your doin', that you killed Two Bear and started the whole ruckus."

"You should have killed him," McCain said bitterly.

"Once I might have," Dannifer said. "But I see what Dan Holder meant about the town havin' to take care of itself. McCain, don't you see how Shute got as far as he did? It's because nobody cared enough to stop him. And I don't mean one man usin' a gun. I mean a lot of men gettin' together and tellin' him he's wrong, and standin' like a wall against him if he don't listen. The town's got to do that, McCain. It's got to sit in judgment on Shute. It's got to go on record as bein' for him or against him."

"And I have to stand with him?" McCain said, making a question of it.

"That's about it," Dannifer said. "Man, there's all kinds of guilt, all kinds of reasons for a man doin' what he does. People will understand that. But you've got to face up to it. You've got to come out and admit responsibility."

"That's a hard thing," he said. "Very hard." He looked at Tammy. "Is that what you'd want me to do?"

"I'd be proud of you, pa."

McCain sighed. "It'll break mother's heart. All right, I'll be ready for whatever comes."

"Better get some rest now," Dannifer said, moving to the door; he let Tammy out, then said, "You did fine in Shute's camp, McCain. Real fine."

He stepped into the hall and found Tammy there. She quickly put her arms around him and kissed him. "Thanks for saying that, Pete."

"I said it because it was so."

"He needed that. He may even grow strong now."

Chapter 19

Pete Dannifer's return to Salem created a stir, and since the town lacked a decent jail the two prisoners were locked in the vault room of the bank. Huber objected to this; he didn't want anyone in there with his money, but Dannifer pointed out that since the men couldn't get out, it wouldn't hurt anything if they counted it to pass the time.

He had his way with the banker, for he pushed and forced it on Huber. Regan and Thursday rode to Portland to bring back a judge; and Dan Holder, who knew something of law, agreed to draw up the indictment and present it to the court. He also agreed to act as the prosecutor for the town.

Angus McCain, unable to travel, remained at the stage stop, and Dannifer knew he would appear as soon as he could travel. He and Tammy rode out to the McCain place;

it was a duty call, unpleasant, and they both left with the feeling that their time had been wasted.

Mrs. McCain blamed Tammy for everything that had happened, and talk only made it worse. Quincy seemed to understand how things were, and gave them the assurance that he would take care of things until his father got back.

They returned to town, and in the morning Dannifer went to his saw camp; there was still work to be done and he had been away too long as it was. They completed the buildings —a cookhouse and a bunkhouse to accommodate the men they would have to hire—and every evening he rode to town to see how Tammy was getting along with her restaurant.

Two carpenters were kept busy there for a week, and the freight outfit of Early and Cogswell brought her stoves and utensils from Portland. Dannifer was surprised to find that it took eight mules to carry everything she had bought.

She opened the place a week after she got back. There was a double line at the door for breakfast, and by noon she had hired two women to help her in the kitchen and at the counter. This caused an additional stir in the town, for they were both bound girls and Tammy bought their indenture for sixty-five dollars. That wasn't uncommon, but the word soon got around town that they were not bound to her, but were free to pay back the sixty-five dollars a bit at a time. She wasn't sure whether customers came because the food was good or because they wanted to see the first free, self-employed women in the Territory.

Dannifer came in that night and had his meal; he paid thirty-five cents, the same as anyone else did. Tammy closed the place at eight, for there were pies and bread to make for the next day's trade.

"I made sixty-four dollars today," she said proudly. "Tomorrow I'll make more, because I won't run out of pies and bread."

He grinned. "Pretty proud of yourself, ain't you?"

"Yes," she said.

"Well, I am too," Dannifer said. "What are you payin' the help?"

"A dollar and a half a day."

He whistled. "That's man's wages."

"They work like men," Tammy said.

"I wouldn't argue that," he said. He went on, "McGee ought to be gettin' back any day now. We're ready to start sawing as soon as we set up the engine and saws."

"If you've worked yourself out of somethin' to do," she said, "I've got plenty around here that needs doing."

He laughed and shook his head. "Thanks, no. I think I'll go over to the bank and see how our prisoners are gettin' along. Who's guarding tonight?"

She thought a moment. "Perry. He came in for supper and said he had it tonight." She walked with him to the door and unlocked it for him, then took his arm. "A judge can perform a marriage, can't he?"

Dannifer nodded. "I'll talk to him about it when he gets here."

"Why don't we let *him* talk while you stand beside me and hold my hand?"

He looked at her, a faint smile in his eyes. "That sounds like a good idea." He kissed her and went on down the street.

When he approached the bank, Perry raised his rifle. "Hold up there, friend. Oh, it's you, Pete." He lowered the muzzle. "Just fed our two beauties. When's the judge goin' to get here?"

"I kind of expected him today," Dannifer said. "Maybe tomorrow. Can I go in?"

"Sure," Perry said, and put a key in the lock. He went in with Dannifer and relocked the door. A lamp burned near the teller's wicket and they went into the back room and unlocked the vault door. Dannifer swung it wide while Perry stood back, and it was lucky that he did, for as Dannifer swung the door open, Abe Shute made a swipe at him with a bag of gold coins. Abe had expected Perry to be alone; and if he had been, they would have carried it off and made an escape.

Dannifer ducked in time and the bag clanked against the iron door of the vault, then he gave Abe a push backward and started to turn. Neal Shute jumped on his back, a forearm clamped around his throat, and Dannifer rammed an elbow back, caught him in the pit of the stomach and knocked just enough surprise into him so that the grip loosened. Then he threw Neal Shute over his head as Abe came in.

Perry had time to step in, and he jabbed with his rifle butt, catching Abe on the jaw. The man went down like a heart-shot deer, and they stood there, looking at Neal Shute, who was getting up.

"Bad try," Dannifer said. He looked at Abe, at the blood

dripping from the corner of his mouth. "You hit him pretty hard, Perry."

"Meant to," Perry said. "You fellas finished your supper yet?" He was completely unruffled, as though nothing unusual had happened, and Neal Shute swore softly. Perry laughed. "That make you feel better?" He tucked the rifle in the crook of his arm, picked up the tin plates, and went out. At the door he spoke to Dannifer. "Abe won't be much company, sleepin' that way."

"I didn't want to talk to him anyway," Dannifer said. He kicked a chair around and sat down on it. "The judge will be here tomorrow, Neal."

"Let him come."

"Oh, he'll come. There's some good odds goin' around town among the gamblers that they'll hang you," Dannifer said. "Thought you'd like to know because you look to be the man who'll take odds." He took a cigar from his pocket and tossed it to Shute, then lit one for himself. "But I didn't come to tell you that. I just thought I'd let you know that you were outslickered, even if you hadn't been locked up in here."

"How's that?"

"When McGee and Jake Early left town, they didn't go to Portland."

"No?"

"No," Dannifer said. "They went to San Francisco to buy a steam engine and a saw rig." He tapped himself on the chest. "I told Ted McGee where he could buy it."

"McGee didn't have any money."

"He had ten thousand of mine," Dannifer said.

Shute stared, and swore again. "I knew you weren't just a drifter," he said sullenly. "Damn it, I knew it when you stood up to me. A man's got to have something behind him to do that."

"Oh, now, you weren't that damned big," Dannifer said, getting up. "Anyway, I hope you live long enough to hear that saw whine. Somehow it means more to me than seein' you hang. Maybe it's because I like to lick a man on his own ground, on his own terms." He stepped to the door, then thought of something and came back, taking the cigar from Shute's lips. "You might start a fire with that."

He went out and closed the door and Shute threw a chair against it. Dannifer snapped the lock closed and went out to the street, where Perry was standing guard.

"A hard loser there," Dannifer said, and went back to the saw camp.

The Portland judge arrived the next afternoon and the trial was scheduled to start the next morning. Dannifer wanted to get into town to see the man, and he had intended to be there when the trial opened, but he had work to do at the saw camp, and was kept busy so that he didn't get into town until late at night. He met Holder at Tammy's restaurant; it was closed, but he used the back door and they sat in the kitchen and talked.

"I don't know how it's going," Holder said. "Neal's determined to conduct his own defense and his brother's, and he's making a pretty strong plea."

"What plea can he have?"

Holder shrugged. "Nothing we'd go along with. He contends that McCain started the Indian trouble, and that it was through his own effort that it was stopped. He admits that you came along and took it all out of his hands, but that he would have achieved the same results without a lot of fuss."

Tammy gave a snort of disgust. "And I suppose he's laughed off the fact that he had me a prisoner—"

"Neal claims you went of your own free will." Holder scratched his head. "Tammy, there's people around here who don't understand you and don't want to. Most everyone figured you and Neal were headed for the preacher, and then you up and switched to Pete. Then you went into the restaurant business, and more than a few female eyebrows raised at that. The men like a good meal, but they've got wives at home who talk and jabber, and in the end they'll do pretty much as they want. Neal's always been a charmer to the ladies in the store, and by golly, it's hard for them to think he'd do a bad thing. What I'm tryin' to say, Tammy, is that Neal's making you out to be a muckle-headed flirt who don't know up from down." He shook his head. "The first day didn't go the way I figured it would. Nobody's mad. The Indian trouble is over and there's no one riled up, except us."

"Dan, you've got to change that," Pete Dannifer said.

"Well, I'm going to try," Holder said, but his voice lacked conviction, the sureness it had had earlier in the morning.

Pete Dannifer managed to come to town the next day and he sat for an hour, listening to the arguing, and then he left and went back to the saw camp. He tried to figure out what was happening, and it wasn't easy; finally he decided that

Holder just didn't have the physical presence to carry off his words with authority. The man was sincere in his argument, but people were not in the habit of listening to him as they were to Neal Shute. Shute's power carried over to them and they had been taught to believe him.

This trial wouldn't last long, he knew, and before dark he went back to town and had an early supper at Tammy's place. Before he had finished his coffee, a man came running down the street with the news, and it didn't surprise Dannifer much.

Neal Shute and his brother had been freed by the judge.

The Shutes took over the saloon that evening and bought the drinks and the street became packed with people anxious to celebrate. The Indian trouble was over and the Shute power was like a strong rope running through the town.

Later the judge came into the restaurant and sat down. He saw Dannifer there and said, "You must be Dannifer. I'm sorry, but twelve men returned the verdict."

"I know," Dannifer said. "But we'll get him next time."

The judge raised an eyebrow. He was an old man with a leathery face and a thick waterfall mustache. "Will there be a next time?"

"Knowing Shute, there will be," Dannifer said.

"You ought to get some law here."

"Judge, you just gave the power of law into Shute's hands this afternoon." He jerked his head toward the saloon. "Listen to that. That's Neal Shute's kind of law, and none of it is written down in any book. He makes it up in his head as he goes along, and if it suits him, he enforces it."

"A pity, but Holder wanted a jury. Myself, I would have put him in prison, at the least."

Someone came running down the street, away from the saloon. "Fight! Fight!" he yelled. "They've got Holder in the saloon!"

The call was a magnet drawing the people toward the saloon, and they moved in a rushing wave down the street. Pete Dannifer put down his fork and pushed his half-eaten pie away from him and got off the counter stool.

The judge said, "I'd advise you to keep out of this, young man."

"I can't," Dannifer said, and went out before Tammy could run from behind the counter and stop him.

Chapter 20

He had to force his way through the crowd jamming the door, and once inside it was no easier. But he got through to the cleared area on the sawdust, and stopped. Dan Holder was on the floor, conscious, moving, trying to get up, but his eyes were closed, his cheek was badly cut, and he had several teeth knocked out. Neal Shute was standing there, his fists doubled, laughing. Then he saw Pete Dannifer and the laughter left his face, left his eyes.

"Dan," Pete Dannifer said, "can you hear me?"

Holder nodded. He could do no more than get to his knees.

"Someone help him up," Dannifer said, and he caught two men with his eyes and held them until they stepped out, bent down, and held Holder erect.

"Why did you come here, Dan?" he said. "Didn't you know he wanted this?"

"I'm not afraid of him," Holder mumbled.

"All right, you've proved that," Dannifer said. He nodded to the two men. "Get him out of here and over to the restaurant, where he can be looked after."

"I'm not finished with him," Neal Shute said.

"You're finished with him, but I'm not," Dannifer said. Again he looked at the two men. "Didn't you hear me?"

He was hard, harder than Neal Shute, and they left, taking Holder with them. Dannifer looked at Shute. "The town turned you loose. I haven't. You like a fight. I've got one for you. But we'll have it in the street where everyone can see it."

"Why, I'd like that fine," Shute said, smiling again.

"No, you're not going to like it," Dannifer said evenly. "Tonight you get paid back for the arms you've broken, the eyes you gouged out. You're not going to be lucky like Dan Holder; he's goin' to get well. He's goin' to be all right. But after tonight you won't be able to remember even your name. You can hurt a man like that, Neal. Hurt him in the head, beat him until his brains get bruised and he's never the same again. I'll be waiting in the street."

He turned then and pushed his way out, but it was easier this time, for amid the hush men stepped back and let him through. As soon as he cleared the crowd, he turned and went to Shute's store.

There was a light inside and the clerk was closing out the day's receipts; he answered Dannifer's knock, and when Dannifer stepped inside he walked to the bin holding leather gloves and found a pair of cheap, rough-sewn work gloves. He paid a quarter for them, then he went outside and soaked them in the water trough. Then he forced his hands into them, and when he balled his fists the leather pulled them into oak knots.

He went back to the street fronting the saloon and took off his coat and shirt. The crowd was already there, waiting. Someone at the back yelled for Shute, and Neal came out with his brother. Dannifer saw Amos Osman move behind Abe and put a pistol barrel against his back; then he disarmed Abe and held him there.

Neal Shute didn't like this, but there was nothing he could do about it. He stepped down in the street and looked at Dannifer. "I knew if I got Holder, you'd come," he said.

He took off his coat and flung it down into the trampled snow, then rolled his shoulders and stepped toward Dannifer, who stood relaxed, arms at his sides.

Someone in the crowd said, "Watch his feet! He kicks like a mule!"

Dannifer ignored this; he had already made up his mind as to what kind of a fighter Neal Shute was. His past victories, his victims told the story plainly; Shute was a grappler, a bone-breaker; he liked to cripple a man before he cut him up.

The last six feet separating the two men was closed by Shute's spring; he almost jumped the distance, arms flung out to get his grip. Dannifer whipped aside, sank a fist into Shute's stomach, and then smashed his fist into the base of the falling man's neck. The blow was vicious and solid, and sounded like a rock thrown in mud, and Shute sprawled face down in the street.

Dannifer stepped back while Shute took his time getting up, and from all sides came advice: "Jump him!" "Stomp him!"

Shute got up; he had been hurt, stunned, but not hurt enough, and when he came at Dannifer again, he did so cautiously, feinting, with his fists. He swung and Dannifer ducked, and this was what Shute wanted, for he grabbed Dannifer around the neck and locked him tight, putting on the pressure. Muscles straining, feet pawing for sound purchase, Shute put a roaring in Dannifer's ears and began to twist, trying to break his neck.

Dannifer tried to trip Shute, but the man's legs were as solid as trees. Then he started hitting Shute, short, chopping blows to the ribs; he felt as if he were pounding an oak keg, but he kept at it, tenderizing the toughness of the man, and finally the grip gave and Dannifer slipped free. He knew that Shute had hurt him and that he couldn't take that again, so he staked the outcome on one blow, and he put it out, a looper that had his weight behind it and caught Shute flush in the mouth.

The man went backward, fell, and skidded, and before he could begin to roll, Pete Dannifer jumped. He landed with both feet in Shute's face, slipped off, rolled, and came to his feet.

Shute was on the ground, trying to get up, and Dannifer went to him, helped him by lifting on his hair. He pulled him erect, pushed him back until the man came back against a parked wagon, and there he held him.

Dannifer hit him with his left hand until he seemed to get tired, then he traded off and hit him with his right. The crowd grew quiet, and the sound of those blows was like a man far off in the woods cutting trees.

There was blood on the side of the wagon box where Shute's head smashed back against it after each blow, and Dannifer's gloves were slick with it and began to skid off Shute's face.

Dannifer quit then and stepped back, his neck a column of pain, the ringing still in his ears. He watched Neal Shute fall, loosely, as though his bones had melted and let him down.

Dannifer turned slowly; he didn't dare to do it faster. He walked toward the saloon, where Amos Osman held Abe Shute. There was a slack, sick look on Abe's face, and Pete Dannifer said, "This town isn't safe for you."

Abe acted as though he hadn't understood. "Neal never thought he could be licked." He looked at Dannifer. "In the saloon, when you said you'd beat him loose in the head, I didn't believe that. If Neal had said it, I'd have believed it, because he had a mean streak in him."

"I'm goin' to do the same to you," Dannifer said softly.

Abe shook his head violently. "No, I ain't much, but I want to be able to know it."

"Then you're through in this country," Dannifer said.

"I'm through then," Abe said, nodding.

"The store's worth a lot of money," Dannifer said. "It's no good to the town with the doors locked. Amos, take him over to the hotel to see the judge. Find out what can be done to sell it. We don't have to take anything from the Shutes."

Osman nodded. "Who's got the money to buy it?"

"Early and Cogswell," Dannifer said. "I think I'm safe in speakin' for 'em, and you tell the judge I'll back any offer made in their name."

"I'll do that," Osman said, and herded Abe Shute across the street.

Dannifer stripped off the gloves and threw them down, then put on his shirt and coat. He saw the doctor then, standing on the inner edge of the crowd, bag in hand. He said, "You'd better take care of him."

"Somebody had better," Doctor Simmons said, "because he won't be able to take care of himself." He looked at Dannifer. "Did you have to do this?"

"Yes, because none of you would when you had the chance."

He looked around, turning his body in a complete circle to look at every man standing in the street. "Where are the twelve good men who served on the jury? Step out and let me look at twelve good men." No one moved. "All right, let me see six good men? No, not even six? Five then. Four. Three. Two. Let me see one good man? Not one good man in Salem. That's just what I thought." He turned toward the hotel and started to walk. "Get the hell out of my way!"

Chapter 21

They parted to let him pass through, and he had to touch no one, not even brush so much as a coat. Once he made the boardwalk he turned to the restaurant, his step slow to ease the pain jogged by this motion. His head ached thunderously, and when he tried to move his neck it felt as if every muscle, every piece of bone there, had been wrenched loose.

Tammy McCain was standing in the door and she took his arm as he came in. She made him sit at the counter, then went behind it and poured him a cup of coffee.

"Maybe we can live our lives now," she said quietly.

"Until the next man like Shute comes along," he said. "And I suppose there's one on the road somewhere, headin' here."

"The town will take care of the next one."

He looked at her. "You think so?"

"Yes. You got to them, Pete."

"That's good," he said.

She watched him carefully, noticed the stiff way he moved his head, but she said nothing about it; it was his hurt and he would want it to heal without sympathy, for it was part of the bargain, part of the fight, part of the price he had to pay for doing someone else's job.

He slept at the hotel that night, but did not get much rest, for the pain mounted and he lay there until dawn, with hot and cold towels wrapped around his neck. This kept the swelling down, and when he went down the stairs he felt halfway human.

He was the first customer in Tammy's place, and while he was eating his breakfast Ted McGee stormed into town and tied up outside. Dannifer watched him through the window and started to get up to go outside, but Tammy put her hand on his arm and he sat there, watching McGee.

He looked at the sign across the front and grinned, hitched up his belt and stomped in, stopping when he saw Tammy and Dannifer. "Well, now, since you're behind the counter, I do conclude that you're servin' meals." He rubbed his hands together. "Well, little missy, you just set up fifteen plates in a row, fill 'em with everything you got, and by the time you've done that, Jake and some of his men will be in to eat you out of house and home." Then he shook Dannifer's hand. "Say, that's some town. San Francisco!"

"Did you get the engine?"

"Oh, sure," McGee said. "Come on, hurry up with that food. I'm mighty sick of trail cookin'." He looked at Dannifer. "I guess you're ready at the camp?"

The Drifter

135

"Been ready. We'd have had the saw singin' if you hadn't dawdled along the way. You pickin' flowers or somethin'?"

There was noise on the street and Early came into town with the leaders, twenty-five mules in the advance train. When he saw McGee's horse he came in, arms outspread, laughing his greeting.

Tammy's help arrived and she set a table for Early and McGee, and Dannifer carried the plates over and the three sat together while the restaurant filled with mule-skinners and noise.

Early dug into the food until the sharp edge of his appetite was dulled, then he said, "I've decided to expand the freighting business and make regular runs to San Francisco. Signed some damned fat contracts there." He thumped Dannifer on the arm. Then he looked around and saw Tammy hustling behind the counter. "When did this happen?" He scowled good-naturedly. "She'll make more money than me."

Dannifer said, "I got you into the store business while you were gone, Jake."

"The hell! What does Shute say?"

"It's Shute's place," Dannifer said. "You'll hear about it."

"I guess I'd better," Early said. "What the hell you been doin' while we were gone? What's happened around here of interest?"

"Not much," Dannifer said, smiling. "Really not much." He glanced at Tammy and she waved at him, then he motioned toward the platter of food. "Eat your pancakes and ham before they get cold."

"Mother hen," Early said, half under his breath, winked at McGee, and began eating. Dannifer put an arm over the back of a chair and watched them, filled with a sense of contentment he had not thought possible to know. Yet he wasn't a fool who thought his life now would be one smooth pull; there'd be trouble at every turn of the road. When McCain was well enough to be brought back to town, there'd be trouble, and he'd have to step in again to make sure no one did anything they'd be sorry for. Neal Shute had paid, and he'd been the one who led McCain by the nose, incited him, goaded him, used him, and Dannifer believed he could make the people in town see that. McCain's place was on his farm where life was simple, and the man had changed, and maybe he needed the cross of responsibility to bear, a sense of guilt to weigh on him.

Dannifer watched Jake Early and Ted McGee eat, and thought how lucky he was to deserve these men for friends. Then he looked at Tammy and found her watching him and he smiled. There was a woman, he thought, with a man's courage, a woman who didn't know what quit meant. Marriage to her wouldn't be easy, because she was headstrong and she'd have her way when she wanted it, but it wouldn't be dull either.

Dannifer said, "Excuse me," and got up from the table and both McGee and Early looked up, but did not stop chewing. He went behind the counter and untied Tammy's apron and laid it down. To the patrons, he said, "You'll pardon us. We're goin' to find the judge and get married."

They cheered, for they liked a wedding as much as they liked a fight, and perhaps in their mind they allied the two.

Tammy said, "Now? With the place full of customers?"

"Now," he said firmly.

"All right, now then," she said, and took his arm, and they went to the door and everyone watched them.

Dannifer paused there and said, "The place may open a bit late in the morning."

"Why, what a thing to say!" Tammy said.

"It may open late," Dannifer repeated, and the men laughed and applauded.

"Well," Tammy said, her face full of color, "it may at that."

Then they went out and down the street and one man said, "By God, let's have a shivaree tonight." He got off his stool, and it started a tidal wave toward the door.

Ted McGee got there first and stood facing them. He spoke calmly. "Gent's, we wouldn't want to spoil anythin' for 'em, would we?"

The man who had started the rush for the door looked at this mountain of muscle and said, "No, I guess not," and turned back to the counter. McGee waited until they were all eating, then he went back to the table and sat down across from Jake Early.

Early smiled and said, "That little gal's cast iron from topmast to keel."

"Well, that's no pussycat she's marryin'," McGee said. He reached across the table. "Pete's left his pie. I guess I'll eat that."

"I was just thinkin' the same thing," Early said. "Match you for it."

"Done," McGee said, and reached in his pocket for a coin.

ABOUT THE AUTHOR

WILL COOK's lifelong knowledge of the authentic lore of the Old West and his deep love of the outdoors help account for both the excitement and solidity of his Western novels. Born on January 28, 1922, in Richmond, Indiana, Mr. Cook ran away to join the Cavalry in Texas at 16, falsifying his age. When he realized that the cavalry was becoming mechanized and horses were being eliminated from the service, he transferred into the air force. While serving in the South Pacific during World War II, his leg was almost shot off, but he managed to return to duty in Alaska before the war's end. He stayed on in Alaska for a time as a bush pilot. Upon returning to the mainland, Mr. Cook eventually headed West, where, among other occupations, he was a deep sea diver, salvage worker, Judo instructor and deputy sheriff in the rugged Lake Country of northern California. When he wanted to turn his energies towards writing a definitive book on the art of Judo, his wife, Thea, encouraged him to write Western fiction instead. By drawing on his own life experiences and his extensive historical research, Mr. Cook was able to bring the early West to life in 56 novels and approximately 100 short stories in a 12 year span. There are over 1 million copies of his Western novels published by Bantam, including *The Drifter* and *Two Rode Together*, which was the basis for a classic John Ford film. In July of 1964, while building a schooner in his backyard in which he and his wife planned to sail around the world, Mr. Cook suffered a fatal heart attack.